SO-SNAP for Energy-Efficient Data Aggregation in Wireless Sensor Networks

BY

Cian John

CHAPTER 1

INTRODUCTION

This chapter gives the basic introduction to the wireless sensor network, parts of the sensor node, and WSN communication architecture, followed by the applications of the WSN. It briefly explains all the challenges faced during the design of the WSN. The chapter also covers several data-oriented approaches used in wireless sensor networks, including clustering, aggregation, prediction, and security. Further, this chapter also depicts the thesis statement and the summarized implications of the thesis alongside a brief outline of the various chapters forming the structure of the thesis.

1.1 OVERVIEW

WSNs (Wireless Sensor Networks) has become the most commonly used technology of the twenty-first century. WSNs are self-configured wireless networks with no infrastructure that monitor environmental and physical conditions such as pressure, sound, temperature, motion, and vibration in the area of interest. It has a large number of low-cost, battery operated sensors, which sense certain phenomena at regular intervals for a long period and periodically send the data observed by it to a centralized point known as a sink or base station for additional observation and analysis. Between the sensor network and the user, the base station serves as an interface. Despite their small size, four basic components make up sensor nodes: sensors, embedded processors, communication units (including radio transceivers), and a power unit [1]. In addition to sensing, the sensor nodes feature communication and processing capabilities.

Sensor nodes are comprised of analog to digital converters (ADC) along with multifunctional sensors. The ADC is assigned the task of converting the analog or continuous data and signals into digital signals before passing them on to the processing unit. A microprocessor is used in the processing unit to execute operations on digital data such as aggregation and encryption. Radio transceivers are used in the communication module to send and receive data via a short-range radio channel. A sensor node's power module provides electricity to all of the components. Electricity is often supplied by a battery that has a limited power budget. Radio frequency, optical (laser), or infrared transmission media are all possibilities for wireless transmission. Sbatteries, either rechargeable or non-rechargeable, are now the most common type of power supply for wireless sensor nodes. Furthermore, because nodes can be installed in hostile or uncomfortable environments, charging the battery may be impossible or inconvenient. However, the sensor network that meets utility requirements must have a long life span. A full life span of several months, if not years, may be necessary for many circumstances. In some circumstances, such as using solar cells, it is feasible to capture energy from the outside world. However, external power supplies often exhibit discontinuous behavior, so a power buffer is also required. In any event, energy is a limited resource that should be conserved. In wireless sensor network development, energy conservation is of prime importance and should be handled carefully. Additional equipment, like Global Positioning System (GPS) and motors, may be required in some applications to allow sensor node movement and placement. Figure 1.1 displays the detailed diagram of the sensor node and its components.

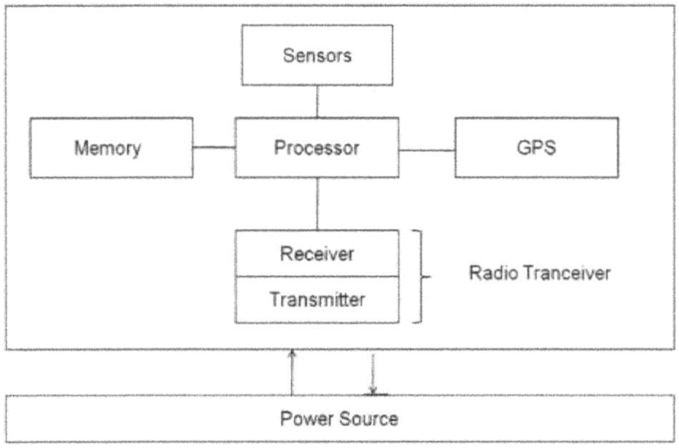

Figure 1.1: Components of a sensor node

A WSN usually includes many sensor nodes established within the utility location and a base station positioned near the sensing location. The base station act because the gateway to the different networks, it sends instructions to the sensor nodes and periodically collects the sensed values of the phenomenon from them. The sensor node locations do not need to be planned or predetermined. In the case of a disaster, this enables ad hoc deployment to inaccessible terrain or calamity relief activities. The algorithms and conventions used in sensor networks must have the capability to manage alone without any help from external resources. Another distinguishing element of the wireless sensor network is the collaboration and teamwork of sensors. Each sensor node has an inbuilt processor, which has the capability to perform simple computations on the data such as aggregation and security of data locally and transmit the processed data to the base station for further computation.

A single-hop network design is where every sensor is directly connected to the sink or base station Single-hop communication-based sensor network architecture is shown in figure 1.2. Even while the long-distance transmission is possible, communication will need substantially more energy than data collection and calculation. Due to excessive traffic and lengthy transmission distances between sensor nodes and base stations, sensor node network lifetime is limited, hence multi-hop short distance communication is preferred as shown in figure 1.3. Because there are so many sensor nodes planted close together, adjacent nodes might be rather close. Single-hop transmission of data consumes more power than multi-hop transmission in the sensor network. Multi-hop communications can also address a variety of signal propagation issues that arise in long-distance wireless communications.

Because sensor nodes are electricity constrained, sending statistics from all of the sensors to the bottom station at the same time is wasteful. Nearby sensors, generally collect redundant and strongly linked data. Moreover, many times the base station face receives inadequate data for processing generated by a sensor network. As a consequence, strategies for incorporating statistics into high-quality data on the sensor nodes, as well as strategies for minimizing total packets to be broadcasted to the sink, are required to save bandwidth and power consumption. The data acquired at the base station is enormous, highly correlated and repeated; therefore, the sink aggregates it and sends just the essential and consolidated data through the network to the user.

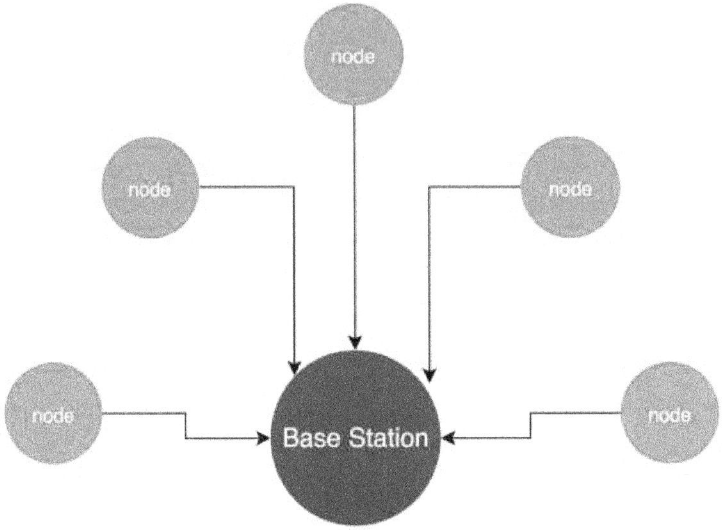

Figure 1.2: Single hop communication

In the last decade, the WSN has gotten a lot of attention from both industry and academia. A lot of research is being done on this subject to improve the development and deployment of sensor nodes due to the growing demand for diverse applications. Battery consumption is critical in sensor networks because the battery power used for communication and transmission is higher than the battery power utilized for computation and sensing. As a result, much more study is needed in this field to reduce traffic and communication in WSNs to preserve power and extend the lifetime of a sensor node. To save battery life, one option is to employ multi-hop short-distance communication between sensor nodes and base stations. So far, various techniques and protocols for reducing total energy usage in sensor networks have been established. The sensor network is a homogenous network in which all sensor nodes have a single CPU.

Computation intensive and information rich applications such as network security, aggregation, and encryption, specifically in multimedia sensor networks and satellite based sensor networks require enhanced communication and computation capabilities. Single core processors cannot fulfill the enhanced computation and communication requirements of multimedia and hybrid sensor networks.

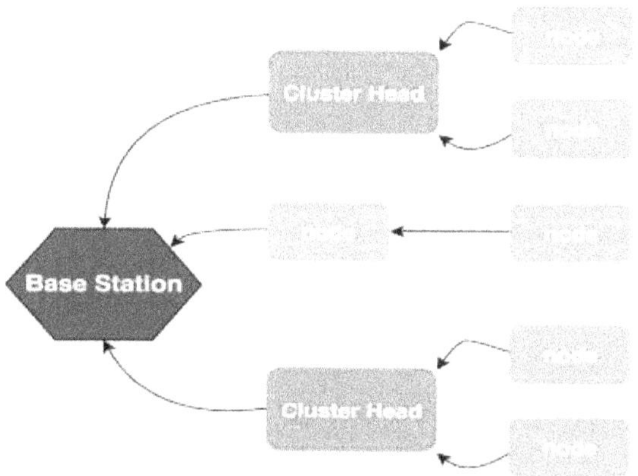

Figure 1.3: Multi-hop communication

Therefore, with the advancement in technology both industry and academia have developed multicore processors for sensor nodes in WSN. WSNs' scalability, energy efficiency, and network longevity can all be improved by grouping sensor nodes into many clusters.

The cluster heads are more powerful than regular sensor nodes, with multicore CPUs and better communication capabilities. Heterogeneous networks result from this type of organization. [2] Describes a framework for heterogeneous and hierarchical multi-core integrated WSNs that can be used in a wide range of applications, from monitoring to tracking applications even in multimedia and video sensor networks. The communication structure of a clustered wireless sensor network, in which sensor nodes are grouped into clusters, and each group has a head node. The WSN communication architecture is shown in figure 1.4. The sensor nodes process the sensed data locally at the sensor node before passing it to the head of the cluster. The additional processing is done by the head of the group and then results are transmitted to the sink regularly, by a no-infrastructure design with several hops As indicated, the cluster head may have a faster processor than the other sensor nodes, resulting in a heterogeneous and layered multicore wireless sensor network.

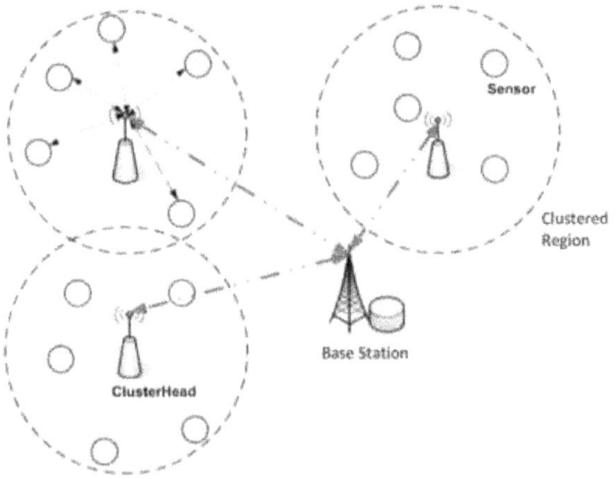

Figure 1.4: WSN communication architecture

1.2 WIRELESS SENSOR NETWORK TYPES

Depending on your environment, the wireless sensor networks can be grouped into five types as given in figure 1.5:

1.2.1. Terrestrial Sensor networks

Terrestrial WSNs consist of the huge number of sensor nodes that are either ad hoc (unstructured) or pre-planned for efficient communication via base stations (structured). The sensor nodes are placed across the application region in an unstructured (ad hoc) mode, which deviates from a fixed plane. WSN has limited battery power, although it is supplemented with solar batteries as a backup energy source. The WSN uses low duty cycle operations, optimum routing, and delay minimization to save energy.

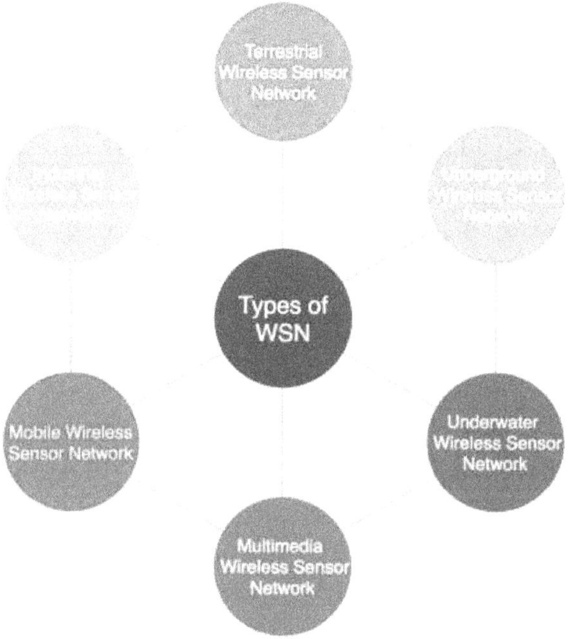

Figure 1.5: Types of WSN

1.2.2. Underground wireless sensor networks

WSN implementation, maintenance, equipment costs, and careful planning are more expensive for underground wireless sensor networks than for terrestrial WSNs. To track and monitor underground conditions, many sensory nodes are concealed in the earth creating underground WSN. Underground sensor networks face difficulty in transporting data to a base station; hence, additional nodes are deployed at the surface to transmit the sensor data to the base station. Limited capacity sensor nodes are also difficult to recharge. Furthermore, owing to the high level of attenuation and signal degradation in the underground environment, wireless communication is difficult.

1.2.3. Underwater wireless sensor networks

Many sensor nodes and vehicles that operate underwater use autonomous underwater vehicles and devices to collect data from the sensors. Water covers approximately 70% of the planet. Long propagation times, low bandwidth, and sensor errors can all cause challenges for underwater communications. There is no way to charge or replace the batteries in underwater WSNs. Energy conservation is a tedious task in underground sensor networks, therefore subsea networks and communication techniques need to be developed.

1.2.4. Multimedia wireless sensor networks

These networks include inexpensive sensor nodes that contain cameras and microphones to allow for the monitoring of various multimedia events, such as audio, video, and images. These WSN multimedia sensory nodes are wirelessly connected to retrieve, compress and correlate data. Challenges with multimedia WSNs include high bandwidth requirements, high power consumption, compression, and processing techniques. In addition, multimedia content requires high bandwidth so that the content can be transmitted correctly and easily.

1.2.5. Mobile Wireless Sensor Networks

WSN mobile nodes can intercommunicate and calculate meanings and they can move independently. Mobile nodes can also interact with the physical environment, making them more versatile static sensors. Among other things, they provide better and improved coverage, increased energy efficiency, and increased channel capacity.

1.3 CLASSIFICATION OF WIRELESS SENSOR NETWORKS

WSNs can be classified based on their operation; however, their properties vary significantly depending on the kind. WSNs are often categorized into one of the following orders as shown in figure 1.6.

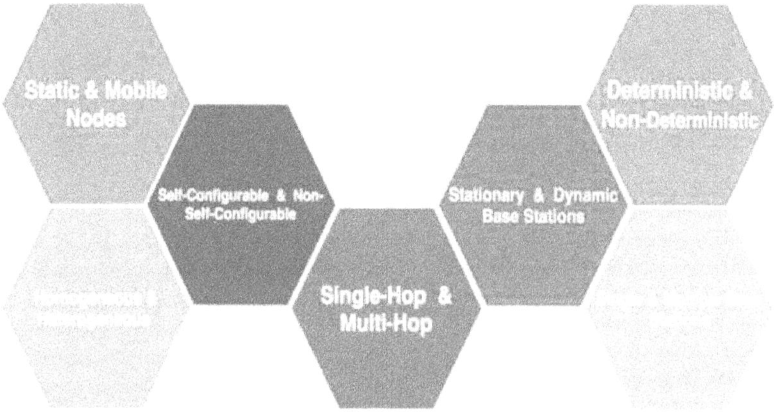

Figure 1.6: Classification of WSN

1.3.1 Deterministic & Nondeterministic

The sensor knot layout can be fixed and calculated in a deterministic network. The pre-planned operation of this detector knot is doable in just a few operations. These networks are referred to as non-deterministic and require a complicated control mechanism because the position of sensor nodes in severe operations cannot be determined due to several factors such as unfavorable operating conditions and difficult terrain.

1.3.2 Single Base Station & Multiple Base Station

Only one base station is used in a single base station network, and it can be placed close to the detector knot. A base station helps sensor pads to talk with each other. A multi-base station network employs many base stations, with data being routed to the closest base station via a detector knot.

1.3.3 Stationary Base Station & Mobile Base Station

Base stations, like detector bumps, can be mobile or stationary. The static type base station, as the name implies, has a fixed position near the seeing area, and the mobile type base station moves near the network making the sensor nodes freight balanced.

1.3.4 Single- hop &Multi-hop

Sensor nodes communicate in one hop to the base station in a single-hop network, however, in a multi-hop network, data is conveyed via cluster heads and peer nodes to save energy.

1.3.5 Self-Reconfigurable &Non Self-Configurable

The organization of detector networks within a non self-configurable network cannot be done by themselves, and data gathering is dependent on a control unit. Sensors in wireless detector networks maintain and organize the network and collaborate by negotiating tasks with other detector bumps.

1.3.6 Homogeneous and Heterogeneous

All the nodes in a homogeneous wireless sensor network have similar energy applications, storage capacity, and processing power. In the mixed network, certain sensor nodes have more processing power and energy requirements than others do. The processing and communication duties are divided into two categories. Enhanced and expanded coverage, increased channel capacity, improved energy efficiency, and so forth.

1.3.7 Static and Mobile WSN

All sensor nodes are connected in a static network, which is used in various applications. Mobile sensor nodes are necessary for various applications, particularly in biological systems. Cellular networks are what they are called. Animal monitoring is one example of a cellular network.

1.4 WIRELESS SENSOR NETWORK STRUCTURE

The architecture of a WSN for data communication networks includes numerous topologies [88] [89], including those described below.

1.4.1. Point to Point Network Topology

There is no center point in this topology. A node can communicate with another node directly as shown in figure 1.7. The most popular architecture, with a single data communication channel that provides a secure communication method. In it, each device may function as both a client and a server.

Figure 1.7: Point to point topology

1.4.2 Star Topology

In a star network, each node communicates with a gateway directly. Messages from several remote nodes can be sent and received using a single gateway as shown in figure 1.8. Star topologies have no way for nodes to communicate with one another. Gateway-to-distant-node communication is now possible with low latency (base station). Because a single node maintains the network, all individual nodes must be within the radio range of the gateway. The benefit is that the remote nodes' power consumption may be reduced and readily controlled. The number of links to the hub determines the network's size.

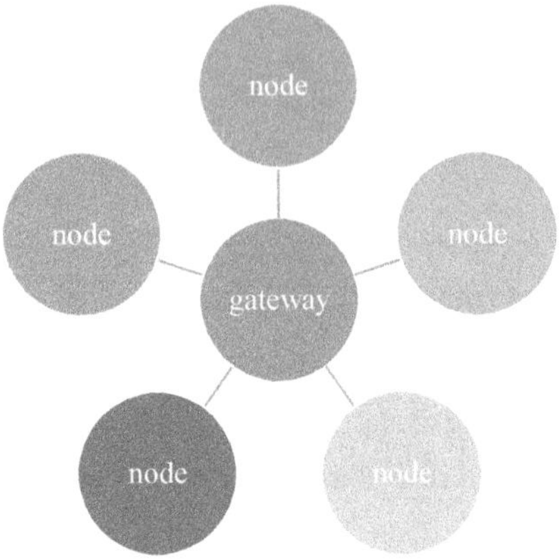

Figure 1.8: Star topology

1.4.3 Tree Topology

Each node in a tree topology connects to a member higher up the tree before connecting to the gateway as shown in figure 1.9. The key benefit of the tree topology is how simple it is to expand a network and how simple it is to find weaknesses. The disadvantage of this network is that it is very reliant on the bus cable; if the bus cable fails, the entire system will come crashing down.

1.4.4 Mesh Topology

In mesh topology the sensor nodes are connected in the form of a 2-dimensional array, one sensor node can send data to four other adjacent nodes within its radio range as shown in figure 1.10. Multi-hop communication is possible because of this. When a node wants to send a message to other nodes outside its range, the intermediary nodes are used. Redundancy and scalability are provided by this setup. This type of topology is fault-tolerant, as a failure of one node does not affect the complete network, a node can relay the message in a sequential way to the supplied destination. The mesh topology is scalable to accommodate new nodes in the system easily.

1.4.5 Bus topology

A node transmits a broadcast message to all other nodes on the network under this topology, but only the intended recipient accepts it as shown in figure1.11. The message is processed. It is simple

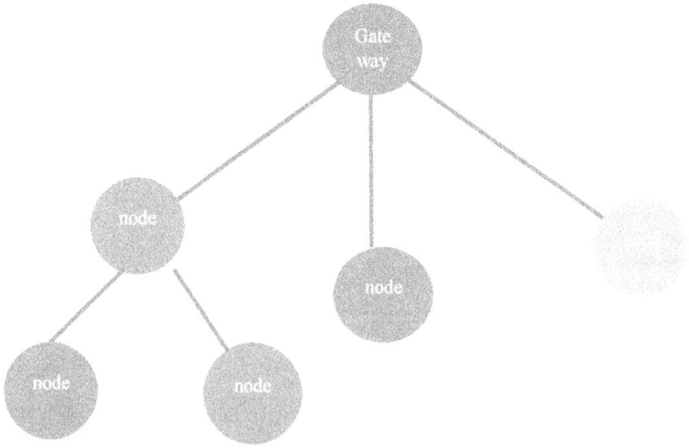

Figure 1.9: Tree topology

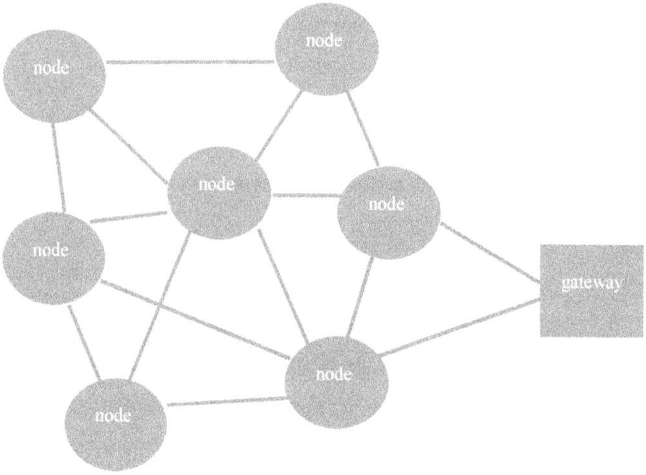

Figure 1.10: Mesh topology

to set up a bus topology, but it is not for everyone. Traffic jams and communication on a single path, however, with a limited number of nodes, bus networks perform best. If a network bus has more than a few dozen nodes, performance suffers.

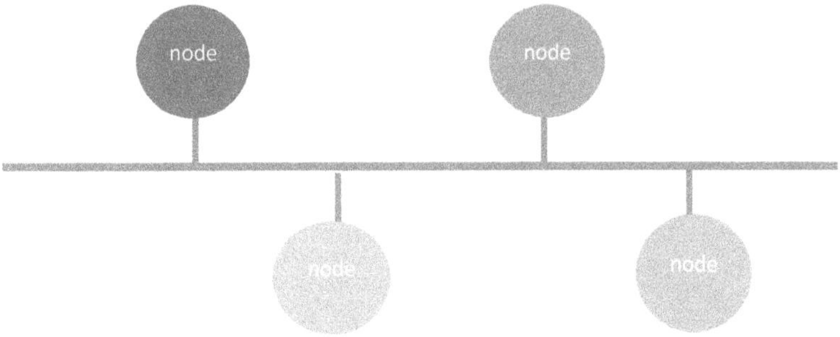

Figure 1.11: Bus topology

1.4.6 Ring Topology: A ring topology is a network setup that creates a circular data flow via device connections. For communication purposes, each node in a ring network has exactly two neighbors as shown in figure 1.12. All communications are sent in the same direction (clockwise or counterclockwise) through a ring. When a node fails, the loop is broken, and the network is brought to a halt. The token is accessible to all Ring devices, giving them the power to broadcast. Because of the unidirectional Ring, a data token must pass through all nodes... When compared to the bus topology, it has a slower performance. All nodes must be turned on for them to connect.

1.4.7 Grid Topology

As shown in Fig. 1.13, the sensor network field is divided into grids. A square grid of non-overlapping squares of the same dimension divides the network region. Each grid should contain at least one and only one operable node at any given moment. A grid's components must work together to extend the network's lifespan. Within each grid, one node is designated as the grid head, and it is responsible for delivering route discovery information and transmitting data packets. The routing is done in a grid-by-grid manner. The grid must adjust to shifting from a centralized to a distributed architecture capable of dynamically absorbing a variety of energy sources.

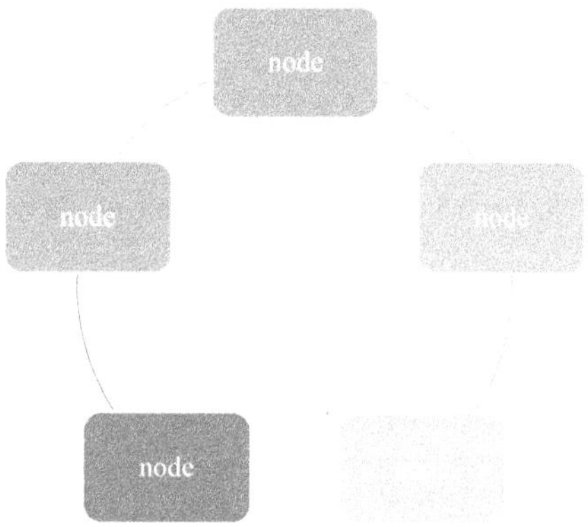

Figure 1.12: Ring topology

Additional remote sensing devices able to measure, track, and share energy data are necessary in order to build a self-healing grid, raise overall efficiency, and increase the level of self-monitoring and judgment. The integrated mobile grid establishes a transmission network that connects all energy-related equipment in the future.

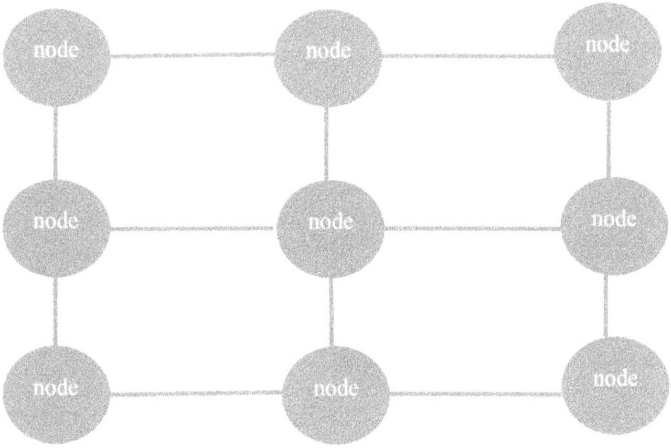

Figure 1.13: Grid topology

1.4.8. Circular Topology

This topology has a circular sensing region with a sink in the center. The sink receives information from the sensor nodes after they notice an interesting event. The nodes are randomly dispersed with consistent density all around the sink, as shown in Figure 1.14. Based on the distance between sensors and the communication range of the sensors, data must travel single or multiple hops before reaching the sink. It is easier to set up and maintain a circular web architecture, and it is more efficient.

1.4.9. Hybrid Star

A hybrid star is a network that combines a star network and a mesh network to produce a resilient and versatile communication network while minimizing the wireless sensor node's power consumption. The sensor nodes with the lowest power in the network topology are not given the capacity to forward messages. As a result, you can reduce your energy consumption. The multi-hop capability allows other nodes in the network to pass messages from low-powered nodes to other nodes in the network. The electricity line is frequently connected.

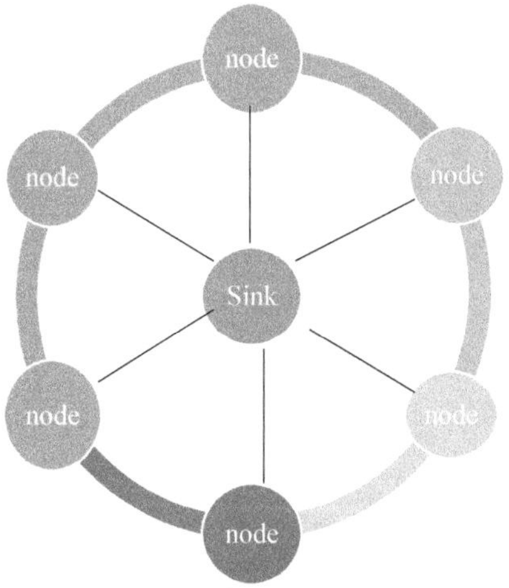

Figure 1.14: Circular topology

1.5 WIRELESS SENSOR NETWORK APPLICATIONS

The WSN's today are used in almost all areas from health care, home intelligence application, environmental monitoring, military tracking and positioning to localization and logistics and so on. It is critical to emphasize that the application has a significant impact on the wireless technology to be employed. After the application requirements have been established, the designer must choose the technology that will allow these needs to be met. The applications of WSN [3][86][87] are of two types, first is monitoring the phenomenon also known as spatial process estimation and the second application is tracking the vehicles, animals, and humans, etc., also known as event detection.

Table 1.1 gives an exhaustive list of the major applications of Wireless sensor networks in tabular form.

1.5.1 Military applications

Sensor networks are a viable sensing approach for military control, command, computing, communications, surveillance, intelligence, targeting, and reconnaissance, because of their Self-organization, fault tolerance, and quick deployment. In the military, the less costly sensor nodes are densely deployed. In case of failure of a few nodes by enemies, the network functionality is not affected. In the military, sensor networks are used to monitor allied troops, vehicles, and weapons, as well as battlefield observation, for disaster assessment, and detection of nuclear, biological, and chemical attacks.

- **Maintaining a close eye on allied forces, vehicles, and weapons**: Leaders and commanders can hire sensor networks to continuously screen the fame of friendly troops, in addition to the pleasant and availability of guns and ammunition at the battlefield. Small sensors may be installed on each troop, vehicle, piece of equipment, and key guns to document their fame. These reviews are brought to troop leaders and accumulated in sink nodes. The records also can be mixed with records from different devices at every stage and supplied to better tiers of leadership.
- **Surveillance in the battlefield**: Critical terrains, roads, and straits may be protected speedy with sensor networks and carefully monitored for opposing forces' activity. New sensor

networks for battlefield surveillance can be installed at any time as operations progress and new operational plans are prepared.

- **Targeting**: The Sensor nodes in the network can be combined into intelligent immunization guiding systems.
- **Assessment of Damage in battle**: Sensor networks can be installed in the target region just before or after attacks to collect the assessment data of damage during the fight.
- **Identification and reconnaissance of nuclear, biological, and chemical attacks**: Being close to ground zero is critical in chemical and biological warfare for precise and fast agent's identification. Sensor networks installed as a warning system in the friendly territory can provide critical reaction time, significantly reducing losses. Nuclear assaults could be detected and tracked using sensor networks.

1.5.2 Environmental Applications

Earth surveillance, planetary investigation, environmental sensing in marine, soil, atmospheric environments, and forest fire warning are just a handful of the sensor networks applications as mentioned below:

- **Forest fire detection**: End users can receive information on the exact origin of a fire before it spreads uncontrollably because sensor nodes can be randomly and densely planted in a forest. Using radio frequencies and optical systems, many sensor nodes may be deployed and integrated. As the sensors are deployed in isolated and unattended areas for months or even years, they could be outfitted with efficient power scavenging mechanisms like solar cells. The sensor nodes will work together to do distributed sensing and overcome impediments such as trees and rocks in sensors' lines of sight.
- **Air and Water Quality Monitoring:** Sensor nodes are deployed in the application area to be monitored. When the sensor nodes identify an event (such as a change in temperature or pressure), the information is delivered to one of the base stations, which subsequently performs the necessary steps... Environmental monitoring also includes oceans, seas, glaciers, the atmosphere, volcanoes, and forests. However, certain biosensors have been created for agricultural and environmental sustainability applications. Air pollution

monitoring and management, forest fire detection, monitoring and management of greenhouse gas, and landslide detection and prevention are all critical issues.

- **Habitat monitoring:** Habitat monitoring is one of the most significant parts of environmental monitoring. A habitat is a natural environment in which an animal or plant grows or lives. As a result, habitat monitoring is critical to ensure their species' autonomy and to avoid any ecological disruption for animals and plants. Pollution can harm one's health as well as the natural equilibrium of the environment. As a result, it is critical to run a system that can track pollution and keep it under control. Design a web-based graphical user interface for efficiently managing pollution data.
- **Disaster monitoring**: In the event of a crisis, a good search and rescue system with a high level of precision speed, and safety for both the victims and the rescuers is critical. Wireless Sensor Networks (WSNs) have recently matured to the point that they may now be used as one of the enabling technologies for catastrophe early-warning systems, rather than just fine-grained continuous monitoring platforms. WSNs' event detection capabilities can be extremely useful and important for (near) real-time detection of meteorological natural hazards such as floods.

1.5.3 Health Care Applications

One of the health applications for sensor networks is to track and monitor doctors and patients inside a hospital. Tele monitoring of human physiological data, administration of medicines on patients are some of the applications of WSN in health care:

- **Human physiological data tele monitoring:** Sensor networks can collect physiological data that can be saved and used for medical research over time. The sensor nodes that have been deployed can also track and monitor the behavior of older individuals. These little sensor nodes give the subject more mobility and allow clinicians to detect pre-defined illnesses earlier. In addition, when compared to treatment centers, they provide a better quality of life for the clients.
- **Identification and monitoring doctors and patients**: Each patient is fitted with compact and lightweight sensor nodes, where every sensor node has a distinct function. For example, blood pressure and heart rate. Doctors can also use sensors to locate themselves in the hospitals

- **Administration of Drugs**: Adding sensor nodes to medications reduces the chance of receiving and distributing the incorrect drug to patients. Because patients will be equipped with sensor nodes that identify allergies and prescription drugs. It has been demonstrated that computerized systems can help to lessen the occurrence of adverse medication responses.

1.5.4 Home intelligence and surveillance

- **Home Automation:** Sensor networks are used in home automation by placing Smart sensors and actuators in appliances such as refrigerators, washing machines, vacuum cleaners, and microwave ovens. The sensor nodes in household appliances can interact with one another and with the rest of the world through the internet. They make it easier for end users to operate their home gadgets both locally and remotely.
- **Smart Home:** Sensor nodes can be integrated into furniture and appliances and communicate with another sensor in the server room and provide, services such as printing, scanning, and faxing. Control theory models can be used to connect these room servers and sensor nodes to current embedded devices.
- **Remote Metering:** Wireless sensor networks can be installed in the home to monitor gas meters, water meters, and electricity meters, and then transmit the data to a remote center for bill payment.

1.5.5 Industrial Process Control [90]

In today's competitive industrial market, industrial enterprises are under pressure to increase efficiency, follow environmental standards, and satisfy corporate financial goals. Because typical wired connections in industrial automation systems are expensive to acquire, deploy, and maintain, low-cost industrial automation systems have become popular, such as wireless sensors are becoming the choice for reducing capital expenditure, operating expenses, improving productivity, and increasing efficiency today. WSN is used in industry to automate several processes WSN is a flexible, robust, and limited system that can be tailored to match the demands of each industry and modified easily in the future. WSN can also be used in inventory control management in the industries. A sensor node could be linked to each item in a warehouse. End users can locate an item's exact position and count the number of items. The users just need to attach the relevant sensor nodes to the inventories if they want to add new inventories and can always keep a track of and locate where their inventories are.

1.5.6 Agricultural Applications

WSNs have been reported to help farmers with a variety of tasks, including maintaining wiring in a challenging environment, irrigation mechanization to improve the quality and productivity of farming. which promotes more efficient water use, and waste reduction. Some of the advantages include the capacity to monitor pesticide levels in drinking water, soil erosion, and air pollution levels in real-time. WSN is used to measure moisture in the soil to gain insight into crop growth and lower the production cost.

1.5.7 Commercial applications

Material fatigue monitoring, smart office space design, office environmental control, robot control and guidance in automated manufacturing environments, interactive toys, interactive museums, factory process control, and automation, disaster monitoring, smart structures with sensor nodes embedded inside, equipment diagnosis, and shipping are some of the commercial applications. A few of them are listed below:

- **Intrusion Detection** [91]**:** In railways, bus stations, airports, buildings, subways, and other locations, WSN can be utilized to identify intruders and assailants and issue a timely alarm. Sensor nodes are being deployed throughout a geographic region to detect and identify dangers, and then communicate these risks to remote end users for analysis through the Internet.
- **Structural Applications**: Sensors are used to perceive the vicinity of diverse structural initiatives like homes and different production initiatives like riverbanks, tunnels, flyovers, bridges, roads, and different developmental activities, permitting manufacturing/engineering practices to screen property remotely while not having to go to the sites, saving cash on visits.
- **Transportation Applications**: WSNs collect real-time traffic data to update transportation models later and to keep drivers informed about probable congestion and traffic issues. There are two techniques for tracking and detecting the vehicle, first, the vehicle's position

is detected and forwarded to the base station; second, data gathered by the sensor nodes are forwarded to the centralized base station to determine the movement of the vehicle.

- **Interactive museums**: It will be easier for youngsters to interact with museum objects and learn more about them. These items will be able to communicate with each other through touch and speech. Live reason out activities that teach children about science and the environment are also available. Wireless sensor networks can also be used to provide paging and location services within the museum.
- **Car thefts identification**: Sensor nodes are being installed throughout a geographic region to detect threats and thefts, and to report these risks to remote end users for analysis.

1.6 DESIGN CHALLENGES OF WSN [4] [5]

Sensor network design and implementation pose many challenges and issues, as the sensor nodes communicate with one another across a wireless network with no substructure [4]. There are three major categories in which challenges are faced by wireless sensor networks [102]:

The first one is real time challenges; WSN is concerned with real-world issues. Sensor data is frequently required to be provided within a specified time frame so that appropriate observations or actions can be taken. In accomplishing real-time standards in WSN, there have been few results to date. In order to fulfill deadlines, most protocols either disregard real-time or try to process as quickly as feasible. It is necessary to develop not only real-time protocols for WSN but also analysis techniques to go along with them.

The second challenge is energy management, since sensor nodes are powered by batteries and changing or charging them is sometimes difficult, if not impossible, it is vital to reduce sensor node power consumption such that the lifespan of the sensor nodes, and the overall network, is extended. Due to limited progress in improving battery capacity, the energy restriction is unlikely to be resolved anytime soon. Furthermore, battery replacement is not a realistic option due to the unattended nature of sensor nodes and the risky nature of identifying locations. On the other hand, many sensor network applications require a long lifetime due to their monitoring nature; hence, a key research topic is providing an energy-efficient observation service for a geographic area.

Table 1.1: Applications of Wireless Sensor Network

S. No.	Main Application Area	Sub Areas
1.	Military Applications	a. Surveillance of allied forces, equipment, ammunition
		b. Surveillance on the battlefield:
		c. Object Targeting
		d. Battle damage assessment
		e. Identification and reconnaissance of nuclear, biological, and chemical attacks
2.	Environmental Monitoring	a. Forest fire detection
		b. Air and Water Quality Monitoring:
		c. Habitat monitoring
		d. Disaster monitoring
3.	Health Care Applications	a. Tele monitoring of human physiological data
		b. Tracking and observation of doctors and patients
		c. Drug administration in hospitals:
4.	Home Intelligence and Surveillance	a. Home Automation
		b. Smart Home
		c. Remote Metering
5.	Industrial Process Control	a. Industrial Automation Systems
		b. Inventory control
6.	Agricultural Applications	a. Irrigation Mechanism
		b. Soil moisture
7.	Commercial Applications	a. Intrusion Detection
		b. Interactive museums
		c. Transportation Applications

The third challenge is in the field of network scalability and management. WSN densities can range from extremely sparse to extremely high, depending on the application. Sensor node behavior in these sensor nodes is dynamic and highly adaptive, as the need to self-organize and conserve energy forces sensor nodes to change their behavior on a frequent basis in response to their current level of activity. Since sensor, networks are generally deployed in outdoor locations; direct network management by managers or operators is difficult. As a result, the framework should include a system for indirect remote control and management. Figure 1.15 list all the major design issues and challenges in WSN. Therefore, to fully benefit from the development of WSNs, the approaches must be planned from the beginning of the system design for effectively monitoring and management of the energy source.

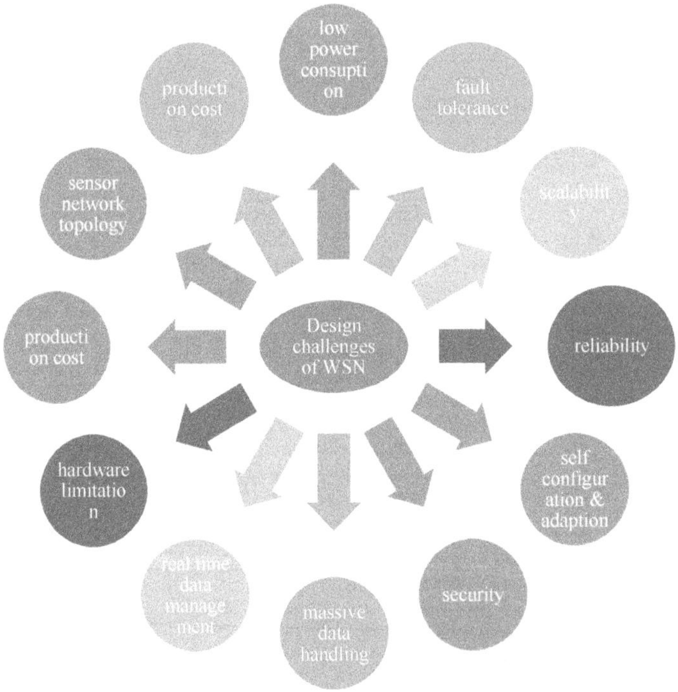

Figure 1.15: Design issues in WSN

1.6.1 Low power consumption: When developing a sensor network, the most important goal is to reduce power usage. Because sensor nodes are powered by batteries and changing or charging them is sometimes difficult, if not impossible, it is vital to reduce sensor node power consumption so that the lifespan of the sensor nodes, as well as the overall network, is extended. Power is consumed for sensing, communication, and data processing. The majority of WNS issues were centered on insufficient power resources. The power source's magnitude is limited by the size of the nodes (battery). As a result, there is a need to carefully consider concerns of resourceful energy consumption while building both software and hardware. The basic job of a sensor node in a sensor field is to detect events, do rapid local data processing, and then broadcast the results. The three domains where power is consumed are sensing the phenomenon, communication, and data processing.

- **Data Sensing**: The sensing power varies depending on the application. Sporadic sensing could use less energy than continuous event monitoring. In determining energy expenditure, the complexity of event detection is also important. Increased ambient noise levels may create severe corruption and complicate detection.
- **Data Communication**: The data communication of a sensor node consumes the most energy. This includes data transmission as well as the reception. For short-range communication with low radiation power, it can be proved that the transmitting and receiving power requirements are the same.
- **Data Processing:** When opposed to data communication, data processing consumes far less energy. In a multi-hop sensor network, local data processing is critical for reducing power usage. As a result, a sensor node must have built-in computing capabilities as well as the ability to interact with its surroundings.

1.6.2 Fault Tolerance: Since wireless sensor networks are installed in harsh deployment environments and unattended operations. The nodes failures are much higher in sensor networks. Therefore, the nodes should have abilities to self-testing, self-repairing, and self-recovering from failures. Sensor nodes in WSN may fail due to a lack of power, physical damage, or environmental interference. The wireless sensor network should not be affected by the faults and failures in the sensor nodes. This is a fault tolerance or dependability issue. Fault tolerance refers to the capacity to maintain sensor network functionality in the face of failures. Protocols and techniques can be used to control the required amount of fault tolerance by sensor networks. If there is little interference in the environment where the sensor nodes are installed, the protocols can be relaxed.

1.6.3. Scalability: Scalability is an important consideration when developing wireless sensor networks (WSNs) routing protocol. A perfect routing protocol must be scalable as well as adaptable to changes in network topology. As a result, scalable protocols should perform well as the network grows in size or the workload increases. Network protocols should be scalable to different network sizes. The number of sensor nodes used to investigate a phenomenon could be hundreds or thousands. Depending on the application, the number might approach millions of dollars. This number of nodes must be accommodated by the new schemes. They must also make use of the sensor networks' high density.

1.6.4 Reliability: Wireless sensor networks have a tough time delivering trustworthy data due to the error-prone nature of wireless communication and the frangibility of small sensors. Sensor networks need to have error detection and correction methods in place to provide accurate data delivery.

1.6.5 Self-Configuration and Adaptation: In the situation of network dynamics and node failures, sensor devices should be able to self-organize and alter their connectivity within a communication network and reconfigure their connectivity. Changes in density and topology must be accommodated by sensor networks.

1.6.6 Security: Sensor nodes are vulnerable to adversaries in many applications because they are deployed in hostile environments. In such cases, a sensor network should have robust security methods to prevent unauthorized access or harmful assaults on data stored in the network or on a sensor node. Confidentiality, integrity, and availability are all aspects of security.

1.6.7. Massive data handling: Data architectures, database management, including querying tools, and data storage and warehousing are all covered by data management. Sensor networks generate a large amount of data, so sensor nodes should be able to store and handle it. The sensor network applies data aggregation techniques for minimizing redundant transmissions. The WSN needs to build a protection model for reducing the transmission cycles.

1.6.8. Real-time data management: Many applications are time-critical which require real-time data processing and transmission. Thus, the WSN should have appropriate hardware and software for data handling and processing in real time.

1.6.9 Hardware limitations: Every sensor node must comprise a detecting component (sensor), a processing component, a transmission component, and a power source component. Many built-in sensors or other devices, such as a localization arrangement, may be included in the nodes at some time to aid with location-aware routing. Regardless, each extra feature comes at a cost and raises the node's power consumption rate as well as its physical dimensions. As a result, the cost and power needs of extra functionality must be carefully evaluated.

1.6.10 Production Cost: Because sensor networks have a large number of sensor nodes, the cost of a single sensor node is critical in justifying the network's overall cost. The sensor network is not cost-justified if its cost surpasses the cost of deploying standard sensors. As a result, each sensor node's cost must be maintained low. Determining the cost of a sensor node is tough given the number of functions available for less than a dollar.

1.6.11 Sensor Network Topology: Even though WSNs have advanced in many areas, they still have resource restrictions in terms of energy, computing power, storage, and communications. Among all of the aforementioned constraints, energy conservation is of paramount importance, as indicated by the huge number of energy-saving algorithms, procedures, and protocols established since the network's inception. Topology maintenance, according to sources, is one of the most critical factors that could aid in the reduction of energy consumption rates in WSNs.

1.6.12 The Media of Transmission: A wireless medium connects communicative nodes in a multi-hop sensor network. Radio, infrared, and optical media can be used to create these linkages. The transmission medium must be available internationally for these networks to operate globally.

To communicate and interact among the nodes, radio transmission over the main ISM bands is commonly used. Optical or infrared communication, on the other hand, is used by some sensor networks, with the latter having the advantage of being more powerful and intrusion free. Effective coding and modulation schemes must be used in conjunction with the transmission medium chosen.

1.7 BENEFITS AND DRAWBACKS OF WSN

The following are some of the benefits of wireless sensor networks (WSNs):

- It's ideal for inaccessible situations like over the sea, mountains, rural areas, or dense forests.
- It eliminates the need for a lot of wiring.
- It might be expanded to accommodate new devices at any moment.
- A centralized monitor can also be used to access it.
- If an unexpected event arises that necessitates the additional workstation, be flexible.
- The cost of implementation is reasonable.
- It is adaptable to physical partitions.

Wireless sensor networks have the following drawbacks:

- Hackers can gain access to the access point and obtain all of the data, making it less secure.
- When compared to a wired network, the speed is slower.
- We could not regulate the propagation of waves since it was easy for hackers to hijack them.
- When compared to a wired network, it is considerably more difficult.
- Easily agitated by the environment (walls, microwave, large distances because of signal attenuation, etc.).
- Communication speed is relatively slow.
- Various elements, such as Blue-tooth, cause him to become distracted.
- Still Expensive (most importantly).

1.8 DATA ORIENTED TECHNIQUES IN WSN

Increased sensor network lifetime may be achieved by lowering the power consumption of sensor nodes in WSN, which is the primary design issues in WSN. In the sensor network, energy is used for a variety of reasons. Sensing consumes energy first, followed by data processing at the sensor node. Finally, during the transmission of sensed data from the sensor node to the base station, energy is used. Transmission accounts for the majority of the total energy consumed in communication, and the required transmission power climbs exponentially as the transmission distance grows. As a result, to save energy and extend the network's lifespan, it is preferable to limit the amount of traffic and transmission distance. To protect data conveyed in sensor networks from harm, secure data transmission is required. The various data-oriented techniques [6-9] as mentioned below can be applied to reduce energy consumption and provide security in WSN's:

1.8.1 Data Clustering: Clustering is the process of grouping sensors on basis of the range of sense data or common tasks involved with sensed data. Clustering aids the sensor network's data mining, processing, and aggregation. Clustering is beneficial in a large number of fields, including machine learning, artificial intelligence, pattern matching, image processing, and genetics. The clustering technique is used to improve a large-scale network's scalability, energy efficiency, and network longevity. Cluster analysis has become increasingly important in a variety of studies in recent years, ranging from engineering (e.g., pattern recognition, mechanical engineering, machine learning, artificial intelligence, and electrical engineering), computer sciences (e.g., textual document collection, image segmentation, web mining, spatial database analysis,) and life and medical sciences (e.g., paleontology, psychiatry, and pathology, genetics, biology, microbiology,) to earth sciences (e.g., marketing and business). A competent clustering algorithm can recognize clusters in any shape. Scalability, the ability to deal with noisy data, and insensitivity to the order of input records are some of the other characteristics of clustering methods. The process of data mining is multi-step. It comprises gathering data and preparing it for analysis by a data mining algorithm, mining the data, analyzing the results, and taking necessary action. The data accessed can be preserved in a flat file, a data warehouse, or one or more operational databases. In data mining, one of two learning techniques is used: supervised learning or unsupervised clustering.

1.8.2 Data Aggregation: Because the amount of data collected in a sensor network is enormous and highly duplicated, data aggregation techniques are employed to reduce the amount of data transmitted, eliminate redundant transmission, and bring fused information from the sensor network to the sink. Data aggregation is useful for lowering energy usage and extending the sensor network's lifespan. The advantages of data aggregation are that, using a data aggregation procedure, we can improve the robustness and quality of information collected by the entire network, as well as provide some redundancy. This redundant data occurs in the data gathered from sensor nodes. To eliminate the redundant data, fusion processing is required. Another benefit is that it minimizes traffic. Sensors are loaded and energy is conserved. The disadvantages of data aggregation are that the cluster head indicates that data aggregator nodes provide fused data to the base station. Malicious attackers may target this cluster head or aggregator node. The sink will be unable to ensure the accuracy of the aggregate data provided to it if the integrity of a cluster head is challenged. Nodes that are not infected can send several copies of the aggregate result to the base station, which is another shortcoming of current systems. It increases the power consumption of these nodes.

1.8.3 Data Prediction: It is a type of data analysis that may be used to forecast future data patterns as well as reduce data traffic in wireless sensor networks. Prediction is used to forecast a specific moment in the future. Data prediction techniques are utilized in a variety of fields, including weather forecasting, stock market trading, education, and health care. Data prediction techniques are used to develop a model of the phenomena being observed. The model is deployed at both the sink and source nodes to estimate the value of data given from the sensor node within specified error bounds. As a result, whenever the sink node requests data to be transmitted from the sensor, node, the prediction model installed at the base station will predict the data values and this, in turn, reduces the amount of data sent by the sensor node. The data prediction helps in lowering the energy required for communication, extending the network lifetime. However, these energy savings can only be realized if the model is accurate and captures the observed processes correctly. At the source node, the model's efficacy can be evaluated and validated.

1.8.4 Data Security: WSN is used in regions that are unmanaged, uncontrolled, and hostile. An attacker can easily get access to the network and listen in on sensitive and crucial communications.

WSN sends out a lot of critical and sensitive information. It is crucial to safeguard a sensor network from hostile assaults in many significant militaries and commercial applications, which necessitates the inclusion of security procedures in the network [94- 96]. Security must be incorporated into every component of the network to make a system safe. To detect both trustworthy and unreliable nodes from a security standpoint, the installation devices must pass a local authentication test by their respective managers or cluster heads. The authentication process will identify the malicious node and will isolate it. Secrecy is important to prevent eavesdroppers from intercepting, changing, and interpreting WSN data and capturing crucial information, all packets exchanged between a sensor and the manager.

1.9 THESIS STATEMENT

In the purview of significant needs and challenges, this thesis aims to "To propose Efficient Data-oriented Techniques for Improving Performance & Energy Consumption of Wireless Sensor Networks".

1.10 IMPLICATIONS OF THE THESIS

To analysts. Our research can help analysts with data prediction in real world applications to predict failing equipment or medical condition.

To Enterprises. Our research can help enterprises for tracking behavior for real time marketing, to optimize resource consumption such as energy consumption.

1.11 ORGANIZATION OF THE THESIS

The thesis has been organized into seven chapters. A short outline of all the chapters is given below.

CHAPTER 1: The brief introduction to the wireless sensor network, parts of the sensor node, and WSN communication architecture, followed by the applications of the WSN is presented in this chapter. It briefly explains all the challenges faced during the design of the WSN. The chapter also explains the need for data-oriented techniques wireless in sensor networks, followed by a thesis statement and implication of the thesis.

CHAPTER 2: This chapter gives a detailed literature survey in four research domains data clustering, data aggregation, data prediction, and data security. It also identifies the research gaps in all four domains and states the objectives of our research.

CHAPTER 3: This chapter describes the first research contribution (data clustering) in wireless sensor networks. It describes the methodology and algorithm of the proposed density based data oriented clustering model. The proposed model has been proven effective in solving the problem of energy holes in WSN and creating discrete and balanced clusters.

CHAPTER 4: This chapter explains the second research contribution (data aggregation) in wireless sensor networks. It describes the methodology of the proposed particle swarm optimization-based data aggregation algorithm. The proposed data aggregation algorithm has proven to be effective against standard data aggregation algorithms in terms of quantization error and execution time.

CHAPTER 5: This chapter describes the third research contribution (data prediction) in wireless sensor networks. It describes the methodology of the proposed time series-based temperature prediction model, which is, implemented both at the sensor node and cluster head. The proposed data prediction model has proven to be effective against state of art time series-based data prediction models in terms of the number of data transmissions from sensor node to cluster head and prediction accuracy.

CHAPTER 6: This chapter presents the fourth research contribution (data security) in wireless sensor networks. It describes the methodology of the proposed enhanced version of the AES encryption algorithm. The proposed enhanced AES algorithm has been proven effective against other data encryption algorithms in terms of execution time and energy consumption.

CHAPTER 7: This chapter presents the comprehensive conclusion of the thesis and summarizes all the research contributions. It also gives possible research directions for future work.

1.12 HIGHLIGHTS OF RESEARCH CONTRIBUTION

The proposed RDHC algorithm's highlights are as follows:

- With installation of more sensors near the base station or cluster head, the energy hole problem is addressed by density-based clustering.
- With usage of recursive clustering to create clusters inside clusters, balanced clusters are generated.
- Within the cluster, the average transmission distance between nodes and cluster heads is lowered.
- The risk of a collision is lessened as traffic is reduced.
- Packet transmission time is cut in half since fewer retransmissions are required.
- Data aggregation in the network could be done quickly, saving time and ensuring data freshness.
- Hierarchical clustering is supported, which aids data aggregation in large clusters.

The proposed PSO-SNAP algorithm's highlights are as follows:

- A unique fitness function was proposed for a PSO-based sensor network aggregation protocol (PSO-SNAP).
- The suggested PSO-SNAP outperforms the existing standard PSO method in terms of quantization error and execution time.
- A comparison analysis was conducted using K-means, K-medoid, and simple average across different versions of the proposed PSO-SNAP.

The suggested ODP temperature prediction model has the following features:

- Real-time temperature adjustment is performed based on sensed data, which is executed when the expected value exceeds the tolerance limit.
- Sensor energy conservation is performed by decreasing the number of redundant transmissions to the head of the cluster from the sensor node.

- Our model improved forecast accuracy as compared to its existing counterparts.
- The sensor network lifetime has been extended.

The proposed Enhanced-AES (E-AES) encryption algorithm highlights

- E-AES minimizes the time taken for the substitution byte-step of the algorithm by using the s-box splitting.
- Multithreading concept has been used for parallel programming support.
- It reduces the CPU cycle needed for encryption thereby minimizing the energy consumption.
- Our proposed model minimizes the overall execution time.

CHAPTER 2

BACKGROUND & LITERATURE SURVEY

This chapter gives a brief background followed by a detailed literature survey in the context of data-oriented techniques in WSN. The literature survey is divided into four parts based on the four domains of research areas as shown in figure 2.1. The first section of the chapter is dedicated to data clustering in WSN by giving a background and detailed related work in data clustering. The second section of the chapter focuses on data aggregation in WSN describing the background followed by detailed related work. The third section of the chapter is dedicated to data prediction in WSN by giving a background and detailed literature review in data prediction. In the fourth section background and detailed literature survey of data security is presented. Finally, to pursue research, Research Gaps (RG) are identified from the existing literature, and the Research Objectives (RO) to cover the gaps are improvised in this thesis.

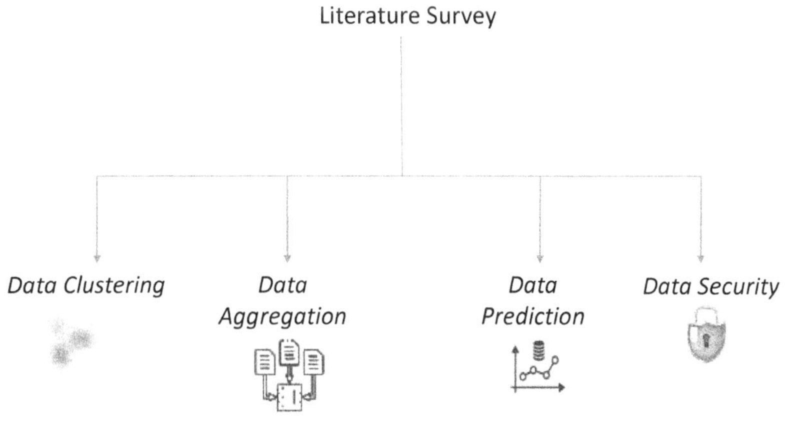

Figure 2.1: Literature survey categorization

2.1 DATA CLUSTERING

Clustering is the process of dividing a data collection into groups of data pieces of the same type. Clustering looks for commonalities in the data items in the input and groups them together. Data points in one batch are quite similar to data points in other batches, but they are not identical. Clustering helps with data mining, processing, aggregation, and routing in sensor networks [10]. Clustering is used in a variety of fields, including machine learning, artificial intelligence, pattern matching, information retrieval, image processing, genetics, biology, geography, and remote sensing. Hard clustering and soft clustering are the two types of clustering [11-12]. Each data point has a chance of being assigned to one of the clusters. Many different clustering strategies have been given, including partitional, hierarchical, density, grid, and model-based clustering.

A WSN usually includes many sensor nodes established within the utility location and a base station positioned near the sensing location. The sensor nodes have the ability to measure a phenomenon, process the sensed data, and communicate information. The sensor nodes' network lifetime is shortened due to high traffic and large transmission distances. To lower the effective transmission distance and traffic, multi-hop short-distance communication is required. In multi-hop communication, data is sent across a series of intermediate nodes, which reduces latency and power consumption while also extending the network's lifespan. Sensor nodes that are closer to the sink relay more data than those farther away. As a result, the energy consumption rate of nodes near the sink is substantially higher than that of nodes far from the sink, and these nodes die off much sooner. This process causes energy holes in the network, which has an impact on the network's performance. Transmission delay and data freshness are two performance metrics that are impacted. Because of the transmission load, data transmission in a large-scale network is delayed. If time is wasted collecting and aggregating data, the value of the data becomes obsolete over time.

Sensor networks need specialized energy-aware data gathering algorithms with high scalability and network longevity. In WSN, clustering is employed to overcome the issue of energy holes. Supervised learning and unsupervised clustering are the two approaches to data mining. [13-14].

- *Supervised Clustering*- Both the input and the expected results are included in this training data. These approaches are quick and precise. The proper outcomes are known and are provided to the model as inputs during the learning phase. Neural networks, Multilayer Perceptron's, and Decision Trees are examples of supervised models.

- *Unsupervised Clustering*- During the training, the model is not given the right results. It can be used to group input data into classes solely based on statistical features. Different methods of grouping, distances and normalization, k-means, and self-organizing maps are examples of unsupervised models.

In supervised learning, the results are known before classification and are utilized as inputs to the model throughout the learning process. These processes are exact as well as fast. Unsupervised learning process models, on the other hand, have no way of knowing what the correct outcomes are during training. Clustering based on data can take several forms as shown in figure 2.2. The following is a comprehensive list of data-oriented clustering techniques:

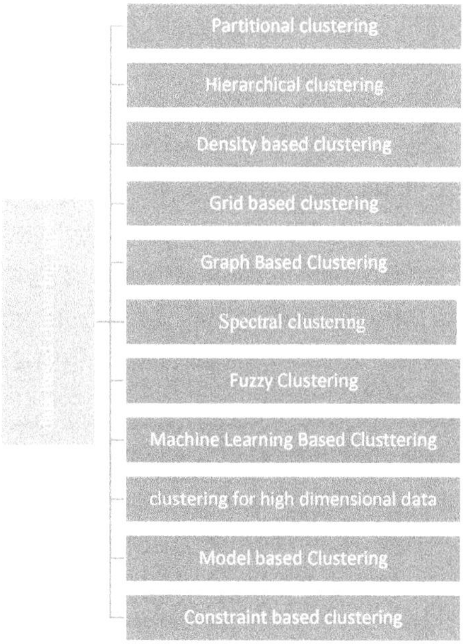

Figure 2.2: Classification of data based clustering techniques

2.1.1 Partitional Clustering

The partitioning algorithm is a non-hierarchical method that creates multiple partitions and then evaluates them according to a set of criteria. It divides a database into a set of K clusters, with the number of clusters determined by the user (K). Partitioning algorithms create different partitions and then evaluate those using partitioning criteria like Globally Optimal and Effective Heuristic Method, which can be further classified into K-means and K-medoids algorithms. Partitional clustering has the advantage of being simple to implement. The disadvantage of this approach is that anytime a point is close to the center of another cluster, it produces unsatisfactory results owing to overlapping data points. To avoid this, the user should pre-define the number of clusters, document partition, centroid position, and iteration number.

2.1.2 Hierarchical Clustering

Using some criteria, hierarchical clustering makes a hierarchical splitting of the set of data. It can be represented as a dendrogram, which is a tree-like diagram that records mergers and splits. By 'cutting' the dendrogram at the appropriate level, any desired number of clusters can be obtained. Sibling clusters split the points covered by their shared parent, while child clusters exist in every cluster node. These technologies allow for data exploration at various granularities. Hierarchical clustering has the following advantages: it does not require a priori knowledge of the number of clusters required, it is straightforward to implement, and it delivers the best results in particular situations. Hierarchical clustering has several drawbacks, including the fact that it can never undo what has already been done, that no objective function is directly decreased, and that identifying the appropriate number of clusters using a dendrogram can be difficult at times.

2.1.3 Density-Based Clustering

For identifying nonlinear forms structures based on density, the density-based clustering technique is crucial. In Density-Based Clustering, clusters are defined as locations with a higher density than the rest of the data set. DBSCAN is the most widely used density-based clustering algorithm (Density-Based Spatial Clustering of Applications with Noise). Density reachability and density connectivity are key ideas in the density-based technique. This technique's key advantage is that it can locate clusters of any shape and handle noisy data in a single scan. Some of the most interesting density-based algorithms are DBSCAN, GDBSCAN, OPTICS, DENCLUE, and CLIQUE. The key benefit of the density-based clustering algorithm is that it does not require a priori definition and can detect noisy data during clustering. The problem is that it fails when dealing with large datasets and does not perform well with data with high dimensionality.

2.1.4 Grid-Based Clustering

The Grid-based Algorithm specifies a collection of grid cells, allocates objects to the appropriate grid cell, computes each cell's density, and eliminates cells with densities below a predefined threshold. It then creates clusters from contiguous (nearby) dense cell groups (usually minimizing a given objective function). A grid-based method employs a grid data format with many dimensions. The amount of occupied grid cells determines clustering complexity, not the number of items in the dataset. The grid density is appropriate for dealing with noise and outliers. It can locate clusters of any shape that are used to store high-dimensional data. The distance computation is not required by the grid density algorithm. The number of clusters is known in advance using K-mean, but the grid density is not. In clustering, the grid density algorithm outperforms the k-mean approach. The grid density approach has the advantage of taking less time to process. The disadvantages include incompatibility with varied densities and cluster overlap issues.

2.1.5 Graph-Based Clustering

Graph Clustering, like spectral clustering, is a simple and scalable clustering algorithm. Between-graph and within-graph clustering are the two types of graph clustering. Clustering methods separate a collection of graphs into distinct clusters, whereas nodes in a graph are divided into unique clusters. There are various algorithms for graph clustering. The approaches that were employed were Shared Nearest Neighbor, Between-ness Centrality Based, Highly Connected Components, Maximum Clique Enumeration, Kernel K-means algorithm, and Power Iteration clustering. It has the advantage of not requiring an initial number of clusters to be given, unlike k-means. Unlike k-means, this algorithm does not require all points to join a cluster. Without any prior knowledge of the data objects, clusters are discovered from the data set. The disadvantage is that because it is based on distance, it cannot be used for pattern recognition in image processing. It creates sharp clusters; therefore, it misses some of the benefits of fuzzy clustering. Because the method has difficulty detecting shapes, it is ineffective in situations when the clusters to be located are regular shapes such as lines, squares, and hexagons.

2.1.6 Spectral Clustering

In multidimensional data processing and data clustering, spectral clustering algorithms use the spectrum of the data's similarity matrix to reduce dimensionality before clustering in fewer dimensions. A similarity matrix is used as an input to calculate the relative similarity of each pair of points in the dataset. Rather than directly clustering data points in their native data space, spectral clustering uses a similarity matrix. In some ways, spectral clustering is more generic (and powerful) than K-means because it can be used wherever K-means cannot be used (just use a simple Euclidean distance as the similarity measure). However, the opposite is not true. The downsides include the fact that it is costly.

2.1.7 Fuzzy Clustering

Soft clustering (also known as fuzzy clustering) allows a single data point to be assigned to many clusters. Clustering is the art of organizing data elements into clusters so that items in one cluster are as similar as feasible while objects in other clusters are as varied as possible. Clusters are identified using similarity metrics. Distance, connectedness, and intensity are examples of similarity measurements. It has the advantage of convergent behaviour, but it takes a long time to compute and is sensitive to the starting assumption (speed, local minima)

2.1.8 Machine Learning Based Clustering

This is a sort of artificial intelligence learning in which computers learn and develop without having to be explicitly programmed. The process of developing computer programs that can acquire data and gain it according to their own is known as machine learning. When it comes to classification, machine learning systems outperform humans. After the system has been taught, classification can be done automatically with little or no human interaction, saving time and money. The drawback is that it is unclear why it classified a document in a particular way, and it is, therefore, unclear how to prevent it from doing so in the future.

2.1.9 Clustering for high dimensional data

High-dimensional data clustering is a type of cluster analysis that analyses data with a few dozen to thousands of dimensions. In domains like medicine, where DNA microarray technology can give a large number of measurements at once, and text document clustering, such high-dimensional data spaces are prevalent, where the number of dimensions equals the vocabulary size if a word-frequency vector is utilized. It will boost the clustering process' performance and give algorithm stability for high-dimensional data. The disadvantage of this strategy is that it is computationally difficult and inaccurate.

2.1.10 Model-Based Clustering

Model-based clustering considers that data was generated by a model and attempts to reconstruct the original model from the data. The model is derived from the data then defines clusters, as well as an assignment of objects to clusters. Neural N/W, Statistical approach, EM, and Outlier analysis are subcategories of model-based clustering. On cluster covariance structure, model-based clustering is flexible. The disadvantage is that selecting a model is often difficult, and data may not fit a Gaussian model. The extra benefit of model-based clustering is that it automatically determines the ideal number of clusters. Model-based clustering algorithms are not without flaws. The approaches necessitate the use of an underlying data model, and the cluster outcomes are strongly reliant on this assumption. The second constraint is high computational requirements.

2.1.11 Constraint-based Clustering

A subset of semi-supervised learning algorithms is constrained clustering. With a Data clustering technique, constrained clustering often involves either a set of must-link restrictions, cannot-link constraints, or both. A relationship between two data instances is defined by both a must-link and a cannot-link constraint. The must-link constraint specifies that the two instances in a must-link connection must belong to the same cluster. A cannot-link restriction specifies that the two instances in a cannot-link relation should not be linked to the same cluster. Clusters that satisfy user-specified preferences or requirements are found using constraint-based clustering. Constraint-based clustering can take a variety of ways depending on the nature of the restrictions. The disadvantage is that not all constraint sets are appropriate.

To detect non-linear geometries, data clustering based on the density of data is highly useful. Varied areas have different densities in density-based clustering, and greater density areas are known as clusters. It makes use of small geographic data clusters. It successfully manages noise in data sets and forms arbitrary shape clusters, which is a benefit of density-based clustering. The density connection or density function is used in clustering approaches based on density. DBSCAN

(Density-Based Spatial Clustering of Applications with Noise) is a commonly used partition type clustering technique [15], in which a set of points is given and the points with numerous neighbors nearby are designated as clusters. Sites with a low density and few or no neighbors are known as outliers. DBSCAN is unable to cluster data sets including data points with large density differences. The quality of DBSCAN is determined by the (eps) and min point's values are chosen. Variations of DBSCAN, such as VDBSCAN, FDBSCAN, and IDBSCAN, have been created to address DBSCAN's shortcomings. The generalization of DBSCAN (GDBSCAN) [16] to arbitrary "neighborhood" and "dense" predicates. The original algorithm's MinPts and parameters are removed and relocated to the predicates.

Ordering points to identify the clustering structure (OPTICS) algorithm overcomes the drawbacks of DBSCAN clustering [17]. OPTICS works similarly to DBSCAN, but it can discover clusters in data sets with varied densities. In OPTICS, the points are ordered linearly so that spatially closer points become neighbors in the final order. Both OPTICS and DBSCAN have the same level of difficulty.

DENCLUE is another density-based clustering technique that creates a grid of data points and stores the grid cells containing data points in a tree data structure [18]. DENCLUE employs two density distribution functions: influence and density. Influence and density are two important notions in DENCLUE. Other clustering methods can be generalized using DENCLUE. DENCLUE is faster than DBSCAN at identifying noise in a dataset. The Ant cluster algorithm [19] is an upgrade on a density-based clustering algorithm that uses swarm intelligence.

In [20], a data density-based clustering technique (DDC) was introduced. The DDC algorithm creates clusters depending on the geographic density of data points. DDC does not require the number of clusters as an input like DBSCAN. It requires the user to enter an initial radius. The cluster head is determined in the first step, and then the starting radius is used to include data points in the cluster. The cluster is refined and the cluster radii are updated in the second step. The user's input serves as a restraint. In DDCAR [21], an enhancement to the DDC method has been proposed to automatically determine initial radii. DDCAR does not drive small clusters into large clusters, resulting in a huge number of small clusters. As a result, DDCAR enables more precise grouping. The DDCAR algorithm does not require any human input in the form of cluster number, beginning radii, or knowledge of data point density. DDCAR only works with Euclidean distances.

AGDStream, MDStream, HDDStream, DCStream, and other density-based data stream clustering algorithms are discussed in another study [22]. These techniques start with grid-based clustering and then find dense and sparse grids by looking at the density values associated with each data point. The clusters produced by these algorithms are pure and accurate. Memory and time are two limitations in these algorithms.

Work in the field of density-based clustering now allows for the clustering of vast amounts of data at a higher level, resulting in large clusters. Data aggregation is not possible with these huge clusters. We require hierarchical clusters or smaller clusters for data aggregation so that data information is not lost during the aggregation and transmission of data.

2.2 DATA AGGREGATION

Because the sensor network's data is huge and highly duplicated, data aggregation is performed, and only the relevant compound data is given to the sink. Data aggregation combines data to decrease the quantity of data transferred from the sensor network to the base station and eliminate duplicates. Data aggregation in a WSN enhances bandwidth while reducing power consumption.

The data aggregation process comprises obtaining raw data from a variety of sensors, using programming techniques to improve the data, and then sending the enhanced data to end users. Data aggregation reduces the load on sensor nodes, allowing for more efficient data processing. Data aggregation approaches have a few drawbacks, such as longer processing times and higher system needs. Redundancy, delay, data accuracy, and network longevity are key issues that each data aggregation technique faces. For aggregating data, functions like minimum, maximum, average, count, and so on are used. The performance of data aggregation procedures is harmed as a result of these concerns. The performance of data aggregation algorithms can be measured in a variety of ways. These outcomes are highly dependent on the application at hand. The following are some examples of data aggregation performance metrics:

- **Energy Efficiency**: Using the data-aggregation approach, the usefulness of the wireless sensor network can be extended. In each round of data gathering, each sensor node should have used the same amount of energy. It is energy efficient if a data aggregation strategy optimizes network performance. The network lifespan, data accuracy, and latency of data-aggregation methods are all factors to consider. These measurements have different meanings depending on their intended application.

- **Network Lifetime**: The network lifespan determines how many data fusion rounds are performed. Until a certain percentage of the total nodes dies, which varies according to the application. If we consider some applications, the simultaneous operation of all sensor nodes is critical; in this case, the network's lifespan is determined by the survival of all the nodes until the specific number of rounds, until the first nodes die out.
- **Data Accuracy**: The total number of readings received at the base station (sink) is compared to the total number of readings generated. Network architecture-based data aggregation protocols, network-flow-based data aggregation methods, and quality of service (QOS)-aware data aggregation techniques are all examples of data aggregation protocols. This section goes through the protocols that are based on network architecture in great detail.
- **Latency:** Latency refers to the time it takes for data to be transmitted, routed, and aggregated. It is possible to calculate the time delay between data packets received at the sink and data produced at the source nodes.

The various data aggregation methods used in sensor networks [23-26] [92] are shown in figure 2.3 and are explained below as follows:

2.2.1 Tree-based approach

This method creates an aggregation tree that contains all of the nodes. The tree is a spanning tree, with sensor nodes acting as leaf nodes and sink nodes acting as the tree's root. The data is sent from the sensor nodes to the root. The technique based on trees is not fault-tolerant. The disadvantage of this strategy is that, as we all know, wireless sensor networks are prone to failure. If a data packet is lost at any level of the tree, the data is lost not only for that level but also for any linked subtrees. This method can be used to create the best aggregation strategies. The maximum value provides the most critical information for the plant's safety in the event of radiation level monitoring in a nuclear power plant. One of the most significant elements of tree-based networks is the creation of an energy-efficient data aggregation tree.

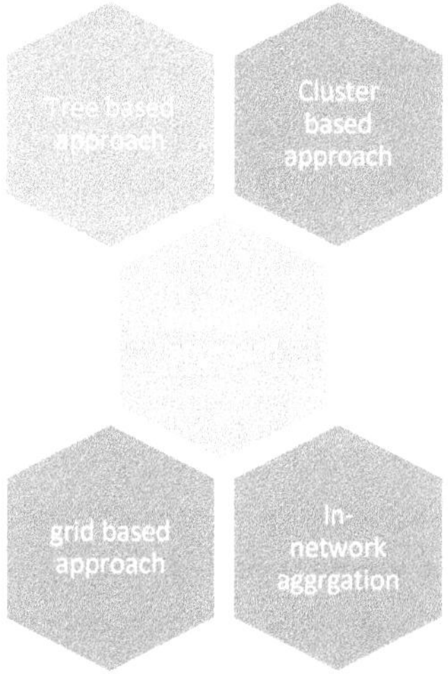

Figure 2.3: Classification of data aggregation techniques

2.2.2 Cluster-based approach

Clusters are formed using this manner, and each cluster is assigned a cluster head. The data sensed by the cluster nodes is sent to the cluster head. Before being sent to the sink, the data received at the cluster head is aggregated. By lowering the transmission distance in sensor networks, the cluster-based method is more resilient and saves overall energy consumption. Cluster heads act as aggregators, integrating data from cluster members on a local level and sending the result to the base station (sink). Many cluster-based network construction and data-aggregation approaches have recently been developed for wireless sensor networks. Cluster heads can communicate directly with the sink by using long-range transmissions or multi-hopping through other cluster heads. A hierarchical technique is the cluster-based approach.

2.2.3 Multipath Approach

The system's robustness is reduced when using a tree-based method. Many scholars have offered a novel technique to tackle this flaw. A node could transfer data through numerous paths while sending partially aggregated data to a single parent node in an aggregation tree. Each node can send data packets to one or more of its neighbors. As a result, data packets move from the source node to the sink node through various paths, with a large number of intermediate nodes between the source and sink nodes, requiring aggregation at each intermediate node. We will make the system more resilient by taking this method, but there will be some additional overhead. The ring topology is an example of this method, in which the network is divided into concentric circles with level levels defined according to hop distance from the sink. A multipath strategy would necessitate the participation of more nodes, resulting in energy waste. Only when there is a loss of data packets in smart data caching, the multi-path is used to implement packets. In many actual situations, only data from a specific circumstance can be acquired. As a result, they take a distinct approach that is based on a spanning tree and only offers alternate routes when a problem has been discovered. For packet forwarding via the network, Algorithm uses a tree-based technique. This is unquestionably the greatest option in the ideal circumstance when no failures occur because the transmission phase involves the smallest number of nodes. In the event of a link or node failure, the algorithm will find alternate paths to ensure that as many packets as feasible are delivered within the time limits. The drawback with this strategy is that it may result in the formation of hot spots, in which nodes along favored paths rapidly deplete their energy supplies, potentially triggering network separation.

2.2.4 Grid Based data Aggregation

Grid-based data aggregation designates a collection of sensors as data aggregators in specific areas of the sensor network. A grid's sensors send data directly to the data aggregator. As a result, sensors in a grid are unable to communicate. In grid-based data aggregation, the data aggregator is permanently installed in each grid and collects data from all of the sensors within it. Grid-based data aggregation, which response to network and event mobility, is well-suited to mobile contexts such as military surveillance and weather forecasting. Grid-based data aggregation, which adapts to network and event mobility, is well suited to mobile environments like battlefield surveillance and weather monitoring.

2.2.5 In-network aggregation

The data collected by the sensor is processed at each hop during routing in a multi-hop network to minimize energy consumption. This method is known as in-network aggregation. In this method, the sensor node having the critical data will aggregate the data packets and then transmit the aggregated value to sink. Each sensor communicates the strength of its signal to its neighbors. The sender will cease sending packets if the sender's neighbor has a stronger signal. The data aggregator is the node with the strongest signal strength after it receives packets from all of its neighbors. The in-network aggregation approach works best in contexts with many localized events.

The cluster and group-based approaches outperform the other data aggregation techniques in terms of longevity, accuracy, and dependability. Swarm intelligence (SI) approaches are evolutionary computing techniques based on biologically inspired artificial intelligence that has lately acquired popularity in the scientific research community for tackling optimization challenges. Swarm intelligence-based techniques are widely being used to solve optimization problems because they provide a superior solution convergence. To solve complicated issues, SI employs the notions of division of labor and self-organization. The swarm intelligence techniques are based on the social behavior of ants, bees, wasps, birds, and fish in groups. Swarm intelligence approaches are used in scheduling of task, load balancing of task, optimization problems, data clustering, and routing of data. The swarm intelligence techniques include Artificial Bee Colony (AB C), and Ant Colony Optimization (ACO), Genetic Algorithms (GA), Particle Swarm Optimization (PSO). The PSO technique is based on the behavior of a swarm of birds or a school of fish. In the topic of data aggregation in sensor networks, a great deal of study has been done.

The authors analyzed and compared LEACH and LEACH-C data aggregation algorithms in their study [27]. The LEACH and LEACH-C approaches are both cluster-based, however, the formation of the clusters differs slightly. Three aggregation approaches are proposed and analyzed at the cluster head level in the paper [28]. The first function is the Jaccard similarity function, which is based on the Set similarity function. The analysis of variation in measured data is the second aggregation approach, and it is used to detect sensors that provide redundant data. The third function is the distance function, which looks for differences across data sets.

The spatial correlation-based data aggregation exploiting spatial and Bit aggregation technique (BAT) combination is presented in a study [29] reduces data transmission by 55% when used jointly. This increases network longevity, and this strategy can be successfully implemented in WSN. Paper [30] presents a data aggregation strategy for WSNs that is both energy-efficient and reliable (EERDAT). The clusters are constructed first, and a coordinator node (CN) is selected to maintain track of the sensor nodes in the cluster. The sensor nodes' data packets are transferred to the cluster head, which aggregates them and sends them to the Coordinator node. The loss ratio is verified at the coordinator node, which determines whether the forward node count should be increased or decreased, as well as the cluster size. This results in lower energy use and greater dependability.

In their paper [31], the authors present a data aggregation algorithm for VANETs that uses PSO to optimize the process of data aggregation in vehicular networks. The aggregate time and accuracy are both performance indicators. The average delay and overall cost of the network are maintained to a minimum. The four goal functions used in the paper are delivery time, bandwidth utilization, information similarity, and information loss. [32] Proposes a PSO-based hierarchical data aggregation (HDA-PSO) for a wireless sensor network. In the fitness function, the residual energy and the mean distance between adjacent nodes are employed. The suggested technique extends the life of the sensor network and reduces its power consumption.

Another paper [33] proposes a data aggregation strategy for sensor networks based on PSO. Sensor nodes, average distance, initial energy, and remaining energy are used to construct the fitness function. When compared to ant colony and genetic algorithm optimization strategies, the suggested PSO-based method is found to be superior to the other two in terms of energy consumption and network longevity. Using PSO, paper [34] presents a new way to cluster data. The output of K-means clustering is used as the initial input to PSO, which is extended to utilize it. To update the clusters discovered by K-means, the PSO is utilized. The results reveal that the PSO technique has faster convergence and lower quantization error.

The authors of [35] presented an energy-efficient and clustering approach for WSN based on PSO. The goal of the study is to increase the lifetime of the cluster heads with the least amount of leftover energy, hence extending the sensor network's lifespan. The fitness function is proportional to the node's average distance from the cluster head and inversely proportionate to the node's lifetime. The PSO algorithm aims to optimize the fitness function's value to increase the cluster head's lifetime. The suggested PSO clustering algorithm is compared to the LEACH, HEED clustering algorithm in the paper, and the new technique is found to be superior in terms of throughput, delay, and energy usage

Another paper [36] proposes two methods for WSN that use PSO: one for routing and the other for clustering. The fitness function reduces the tradeoff between the number of hops and transmission distance in the routing algorithm. The clustering algorithm assigns a lower number of nodes to the cluster heads, which are employed in routing, to reduce energy consumption and extend the life of the sensor network.

The enhanced version of an optimized energy-efficient routing technique is proposed (E-OEERP) in the paper [37]. For clustering and routing, the E-OEERP uses PSO in conjunction with the gravitational search algorithm (GSA). The combined strategy prevents the creation of low-energy nodes, hence increasing the sensor network's life. The cluster assistance node is used to reduce the cluster head's overhead. The PSO aids in the assignment of all nodes to a cluster, ensuring that no residual nodes arise. During routing, the GSA approach is utilized to determine the node position for the next hop.

For the Internet of Things (IoT), the research in [38] suggests clustering-based data aggregation and data encryption approaches. The nodes are grouped using the PSO algorithm in the first phase, and the cluster head encrypts the clustered data before transmitting it to the gateway using elliptic curve cryptography (ECC) in the second phase. The time it takes packets to go from one end to the other, as well as the amount of energy consumed, determines the fitness function. It was discovered that the S-PSO method performs better in terms of propagation delay, energy consumption, and throughput when compared to the Lifetime Maximizing optimal Clustering Algorithm (LiMCA) and the Unequal Clustering Algorithm Concerned with Time Delay (UCATD).

PSO's suitability to address WSN concerns such as data aggregation, clustering, and node placement was discussed by the authors in [39]. These difficulties can be expressed as optimization problems, which can be easily solved with PSO due to its ease of use and better convergence. PSO has been utilized for data aggregation to deliver the best solutions for three problems: optimal transmission power allocation, determining the best local threshold, and the sensor setup. PSO has been in use for data clustering and routing in sensor networks.

The research in [40] has proposed an Ant colony (ACO) based optimal In-Network data aggregation technique for WSN. The paper has proposed two approaches that eliminate redundancy in the transmitted message and maximize the energy efficiency in WSN. One of the proposed algorithms also improves scalability. The authors in [41] have proposed a swarm intelligence-based hybrid data aggregation technique using a Genetic algorithm (GA) and an artificial bee colony (ABC) algorithm for WSN. The proposed hybrid technique creates a data aggregation tree for improving energy efficiency in WSN.

In paper [42] three data aggregation methods such as set similarity functions, distance functions, and one-way ANOVA model with statistical tests are applied in the wireless sensor network. The paper also compares their performances based on energy consumption and data latency and accuracy.

The research in [43] has used a Mobile agent based distributed algorithm for data aggregation in WSN using clustering approach. The proposed approach uses distributed algorithm for data aggregation and is fault tolerant and more energy-efficient than other existing approaches.

Paper [44] has proposed an integrated technique using divide and conquer and enhanced K-means to do data aggregation at sensor node add cluster head level in WSN. The proposed integrated approach not only saves energy but also preserves the data accuracy at the base station.

According to research on the subject of data aggregation in sensor networks, hierarchical techniques to data aggregation, such as tree or clustering, are the most prevalent. The PSO technique has been used in VANETs and sensor networks to accomplish data aggregation over the whole network.

2.3 DATA PREDICTION

Wireless sensor networks have a wide range of applications in areas where people may not act frequently, such as civil, military, and health. The sensor network's nodes should have a longer life span. Many power management strategies are available to extend the sensor network's lifetime by minimizing power usage in a variety of sensor-based activities. Data-driven approaches can be used to decrease data traffic between the base station and sensor nodes. Using data aggregation, compression, and prediction algorithms, the flow of data traffic from sensor nodes to the sink node is minimized. Data prediction techniques are used to develop a model of the events under investigation. The model is deployed at both the sink and source nodes to estimate the value of data given from the sensor node within specified error bounds. As a result, whenever the sink node requires data from the sensor, the model deployed at the sink is used to predict the value of data at that specific instant, reducing the amount of data sent by the sensor node while also lowering the energy required for communication, thereby extending the network lifetime. However, this energy savings can only be realized if the model is correct and accurately represents the observed processes. The model's efficacy can be verified and validated by the model at the source node. The three types of data prediction strategies are given in figure 2.4 and explained below [45]:

2.3.1 Stochastic Approaches

To model sensor network data, stochastic approaches use random process-based probability density functions. There are several models, each of which is reproduced at the source and sink. In this situation, the underlying model is probabilistic, which implies that a probability density function (pdf) matching to a collection of features is obtained after a training period. The source node changes the model when it is no longer considered valid and delivers some samples to the sink, which updates the relevant instance. The stochastic techniques provide a general and sound methodology that also allows for high-level operations like aggregation. This approach's primary downside is its high computational cost, which may be prohibitive for today's off-the-shelf sensor devices. Stochastic approaches appears to be more convenient when many powerful sensors are available. Improvements in this direction could include developing simpler distributed models to achieve the desired trade-off between computation and fidelity.

2.3.2 Time Series Prediction

Periodic sampling and regression are used in time series forecasting approaches to gather historical data series and then predict future values in the same series. Time series are commonly represented using moving average (MA), auto-regressive (AR), and auto-regressive moving average (ARMA) models. These models are simple, yet they may be utilized with great precision in a variety of situations. Even with simple models (low order AR/MA), time series forecasting approaches can achieve sufficient accuracy. As a result, their integration into sensor devices is straightforward and light. Furthermore, until a model is established, most advanced procedures do not require the sharing of all detected data. They also allow for the detection of outliers and model discrepancies. Using a certain type of model, on the other hand, necessitates that it be truly suited for representing the phenomenon of interest. This would necessitate an ad hoc validation procedure, which is not always possible

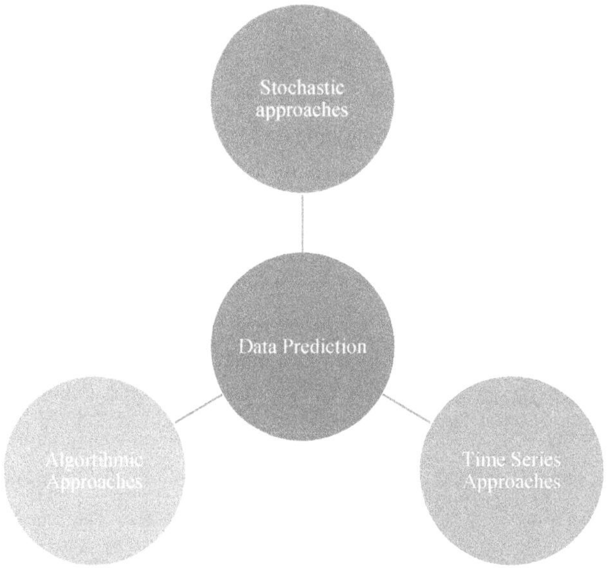

Figure 2.4: Classification of data prediction techniques

2.3.3 Algorithmic Approaches

The state transition model and heuristic are used in algorithmic approaches to characterize observed phenomena. Because algorithmic techniques are more application specific, they must be assessed on a case-by-case basis. To that aim, a research direction might focus on determining whether a certain solution is effective in real-world circumstances for a given class of applications so that it can be used as a benchmark for additional research and prospective enhancements.

Weather forecasting, stock market analysis, customer relationship management, financial banking, education, health care, and other applications of data prediction techniques have all had an impact on human life. Weather forecasting and prediction is a fascinating topic with applications in agriculture, tourism, and airplane navigation. Researchers have been drawn to the vast amount of weather observation data available to create prediction models, uncover hidden patterns, and forecast weather conditions. Weather prediction refers to a short-term temperature prediction that is based on a single parameter (two-dimensional data) and is used to forecast a single instance of temperature, such as the temperature of a specific location for the next instant or a few hours later, depending on the application requirements. Weather forecasting, on the other hand, refers to the long-term prediction of temperature, which could be for a few days, a month, or even a season. The weather prediction is based on several variables (multidimensional data) such as temperature, air pressure, humidity, and other factors, and it predicts various temperature instances over a period of days or months.

This section gives a synopsis of related studies in the disciplines of weather and stock market forecasting. A data aggregation method based on data prediction using the grey model and Kalman filter prediction techniques is developed [46] for reducing energy usage and redundant data transfer in sensor networks. The Kalman filter (KFDA) and grey model (GMDA) based data aggregation techniques are first explained and then a hybrid data aggregation model (CoGKDA) is presented. For synchronization of prediction data between the source node and the base station, the model employs a double queue technique. For testing purposes, a real-time temperature dataset with 720 continuous data points was employed. CoGKDA, a hybrid scheme, saves 35.21 percent communication energy, but GMDA only saves 25.22 percent and KFDA only saves 33.62 percent. As a result, the hybrid strategy outperforms the other two existing methods.

A comparison of deep learning approaches for climate forecasting was conducted in another study [47]. Convolutional Network (CN), Recurrence Neural Network (RNN), and Conditional Restricted Boltzmann Machine are the prediction models that are compared (CRBM). Based on the meteorological dataset provided by BMKG and NOAA, these models are compared against one another. The findings of the experiment reveal that the RNN model predicts rainfall more accurately. In another study, the authors used Hadoop to do predictive analysis for weather prediction [48]. Hadoop is given a vast amount of rainfall data to process, and then the predictive analysis is completed. The chance of rain is then predicted using the lowest, maximum, and average numbers. It predicts rainfall using the Hadoop framework's naive Bayes method.

In [49], the Bayesian prediction model of data mining was utilized to predict rainfall. The Indian meteorological department (IMD) provided the data, which included 36 attributes. The original data collection is preprocessed and some adjustments are made before using the Bayesian prediction model. A prediction model is built using the Bayesian classification process. The test dataset is then used to validate the prediction model. The created model is straightforward and has a high prediction accuracy. The model's downside is that if a predictor variable is not included in the dataset, the model assumes zero probability for that variable, which may decrease prediction accuracy. A new approach for collecting, analyzing, and predicting temperature from meteorological data has been proposed [50]. The Kalman filter technique was used to estimate temperature forecasts for the near term (up to 3 hours). The new method enhances precision and reduces temperature mistakes. The Kalman filter technique reduces bias by 100 times and standard deviation by 20%, resulting in a reduction in anticipated temperature error.

A black-box modeling technique for temperature forecasting was developed in [51]. K-Nearest Neighbor (K-NN) and Elastic net approaches are used in black-box modeling to pick features and generate a sparse model. This phase reduces the level of complexity. Then, as a regression method, least square support vector machines (LS-SVM) are employed to create a forecast model. Only the LS-SVM technique and Elastic net + LS-SVM models were used to compare the prediction outcomes of the proposed model utilizing K-NN + Elastic net + LS-SVM with weather underground forecast. The findings are equivalent and, in some circumstances, even better than those of other procedures.

Another study proposed and evaluated high resolution and now casting thunderstorm forecasting models with existing models [52]. In thunderstorm forecasting, prediction models such as Support vector machines (SVM) and Rough sets (RS) are utilized, however, they lack high resolution and now casting. As a result, RS-SVM, a combination of these two methods, has been proposed. The scheme proposed has been analyzed and tested in MATLAB using a real dataset, as well as compared to the RS and SVM schemes. RS-SVM has a forecast accuracy of 71%, whilst RS (47%) and SVM have forecast accuracy of 47%, respectively (65 percent).

The authors of [53] proposed a fuzzy stochastic prediction approach for real-time stock price prediction. The fuzzy stochastic approach keeps the data in a normal range and eliminates outliers. The grey prediction approach, which is also a real-time predictor, is compared to the suggested method. The grey prediction approach has a departure of up to 6.6 percent, while the fuzzy prediction method has a deviation of less than 4.5 percent, according to the findings. Furthermore, the proposed method is more precise than grey prediction. In a separate study [54], the authors used the Support Vector Machine (SVM)-based machine learning technique that had been presented for stock market forecasting. Because traditional prediction models like regression models are unpredictable and unstable, they struggle in out-of-sample predictability tests. SVM produces stock predictions by analyzing the link between company-specific features and macroeconomic factors. SVM has a 97.4 percent accuracy for training datasets and a 70% accuracy for out of training datasets, according to the results.

[55] Presents a Hidden Markov Model (HMM)-based stock market prediction approach. In the field of stock market prediction, this research examines SVM, Neural Network (NN), and HMM. HMM, unlike SVM and NN models, can efficiently extract information from a dataset and handle market swings better. A statistic for evaluating performance has been the mean absolute percentage inaccuracy. When compared to other methodologies, the HMM model has higher accuracy in predicting stock values of various companies.

A stock market prediction strategy based on connected time series data is proposed in [56]. The suggested method determines the link between the forecasted stock and other time-series data, mainly oil prices, world stock market, foreign stock, and temperature indices. The suggested technique's first phase uses an evolution method to uncover the connection between predicted and other time-series data, and the second phase is the prediction phase. The proposed method is more suited to the manufacturing industry and provides more precise predictions.

Another innovative outlier data mining approach for long-term stock market forecasting has been offered [57]. To create a volume distribution matrix, high-frequency tick-by-tick data from the stock market is collected and preprocessed. This matrix is fed into the Outlier data mining algorithm, which detects abnormalities and groups them into clusters such as normal and anomaly clusters. The anomalies are used to forecast upward stock market trends. The results of the tests demonstrate that the new outlier mining method has a good average return and success rate.

[58] Introduced the statistical Auto-Regressive Integrated Moving Average (ARIMA) model for predicting future stock prices using time series data. The paper outlines Indian stock market concepts and patterns, as well as how to use time-series data effectively in stock prediction. To predict stock market volatility, the study integrates two models, Auto Regression (AR) and Moving Average (MA), producing an efficient ARIMA model. The results show a 5% difference in results. The ARIMA model can be used in a variety of fields, including health care, education, and finance.

To forecast stock market movement, a multi-source multiple instance model has been suggested [59]. This study makes improved predictions by combining data from a variety of different sources, such as social media, sentiments, news events, into a structure and taking out relevant signals from it. In addition, a novel paradigm for representing events is provided. It has been discovered that news events have a greater impact on stock forecasting than quantitative data.

The On-Balance-Volume (OBV) indicator was utilized in research done in [60] to anticipate changes in stock prices. The authors have demonstrated that employing the OBV indicator as a trading rule produces great profitability and returns in stock markets, particularly in China. To forecast stock price movements, OBV uses the stock's trading volume and closing prices. Market reversals can also be predicted using OBV. A CPU consumption prediction technique based on linear regression has been proposed [61]. The authors of the study use the last one-hour's CPU consumption to develop a linear regression model, which they then use to forecast CPU utilization in host computers to perform live virtual machine migration in data centers. In cloud-based data centers, the proposed technique reduces energy usage and service level agreement violation rates.

Techniques including SVM, KNN, neural networks, and the Kalman filter are used in temperature prediction research. Some approaches, such as OBV and ARIMA, are widely utilized in stock forecasting. All of these methods and models employ training data to build a model, which is then used with test data to predict future values, with no real-time adjustments with real data if the tolerance limit is exceeded. As a result, a prediction model that can perform data prediction and real-time adaptation of real data values is required.

2.4 DATA SECURITY

As wireless networks are open networks, anyone, including attackers, can easily break in and listen in on vital and sensitive communications via the radio interface. As a result, security procedures in WSN are crucial for protecting data from hostile attacks [101]. The deployment sensors have to pass a node authentication examination conducted by the head of the clusters to detect both trustworthy and not reliable nodes from a security viewpoint, and all the nodes that have failed the authentication test are isolated from WSNs. All packets transmitted between a sensor and the cluster head or the base station node must be kept secret to avoid eavesdroppers from intercepting, altering, and analyzing WSN data and collecting important information. The primary security needs of WSN are depicted in figure 2.5 and explained below [62, 63]:

2.4.1 Data Confidentiality

It ensures that data and communication are kept secret from any unauthorized access. Other than the recipient, no one else should hear and understand the message, according to the security system. Sensor readings should not be leaked to other networks via a sensor network. Nodes can exchange highly sensitive data in a variety of applications. That one common method for keeping sensitive material private is to encrypt it using a secret key that only the intended recipients have access to, thereby ensuring confidentiality. Data confidentiality is a fundamental security concept that appears in practically every security protocol.

2.4.2 Data Integrity

Moving on to the integrity goal, data exchanged via insecure networks are vulnerable to interception. Because the repercussions of employing erroneous information might be severe, such as in the healthcare profession, where lives are at stake, a lack of integrity can generate a slew of issues. Integrity protection must be applied to ensure that data is not tampered with in any way. The message's data integrity ensures that it is not tampered with during transmission. Many sensor applications, such as pollution and healthcare monitoring, rely on data integrity to produce accurate results; it would be unacceptable to measure the magnitude of pollution caused by chemical waste only to later discover that the data provided by a factory near the monitored lake was improperly manipulated. As a result, it is critical to ensure that data gets from point A to point B without being intercepted or altered.

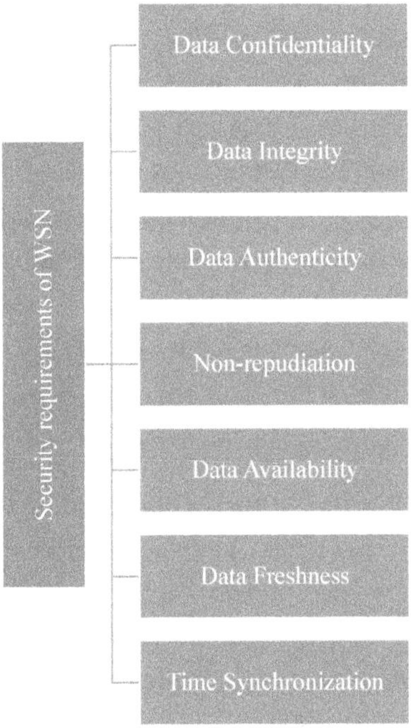

Figure 2.5: Security requirements of WSN

2.4.3 Data Authenticity

In sensor networks, each sensor node and the base station must be able to verify that the data received was delivered by a trusted sender and not by an attacker who misled genuine nodes into accepting fake data. If this occurs and erroneous data is sent into the network, the network's behavior cannot be predicted and will, in most cases, not turn out as planned. When clustering nodes, the authentication goal is critical to achieving. Clustering is the practice of grouping nodes together based on some property, such as their location, sensing data, or other criteria, and each cluster typically has a cluster head. The cluster head is the node that links the cluster to the remainder of the sensor network (meaning that the cluster heads serve as a conduit for communication between distinct clusters.). There are two authentication possibilities to consider when clustering is required. To begin, it is vital to make sure that nodes in each cluster only share data with authorized nodes that the cluster trusts. Otherwise, if nodes inside a cluster analyze data from nodes outside the current community of nodes, the expected data from that cluster will be based on incorrect data, which could result in damage. The second authentication scenario comprises communication between each cluster's cluster leaders; only cluster heads who can authenticate their identities should be contacted. No hostile node should be able to connect to a legitimate cluster head and broadcast false data or compromise shared data.

2.4.4 Non-repudiation

It means that neither the sender nor the receiver will be able to deny that the message was transmitted or received. Non-repudiation is the assurance that one cannot refute the legitimacy of anything. Non-repudiation is a legal notion that is commonly used in the world of information security to describe a service that verifies the origin and integrity of data. Non-repudiation, in other words, makes disputing who/where a message came from, as well as its legitimacy and integrity, nearly impossible. Digital signatures can provide non-repudiation in online transactions when used in conjunction with other security measures, which is required to ensure that a party to an agreement or communication cannot deny the authenticity of their signature on a document or the communication itself. The capacity to verify that a party to a contract or communication recognizes the authenticity of their signature on a document or the delivery of a message is referred to as non-repudiation in this context.

2.4.5. Data Availability

Data Availability is a guarantee that services and information are always available many threats to sensor networks, such as sensor node capture and denial-of-service attacks can cause them to go down. Lack of availability can disrupt the operation of many critical real-time applications, such as those in the healthcare industry that must operate 24 hours a day, seven days a week, and can even result in death. As a result, it is critical to ensure system availability resilience and find ways to bridge the gap left by a given node's capture or disablement by delegating its functions to other nodes in the network. It ensures that all services are available to users in all circumstances.

2.4.6 Data Freshness

Data freshness ensures that data received at the node is current and accurate for the time specified. The message replay attack is one of several types of sensor network assaults in which an adversary intercepts messages exchanged between nodes and replays them later to mislead the network. The data freshness goal ensures that messages are fresh in the sense that they have not been repeated and follow a message ordering. To keep network protocols fresh, duplicate packets must be recognized and deleted, preventing any mix-ups.

2.4.7 Time Synchronization

The majority of remote sensing applications depend on time synchronization in some way. The radio of a single sensor can be turned off for short periods to save electricity. Additionally, sensors may want to calculate the packet's end-to-end delay as it travels between two paired sensors. For tracking applications, etc., a more collaborative sensor network may necessitate group synchronization.

Sensor networks are especially sensitive to many different sorts of attacks. Denial of service attacks, for example, can be carried out in a variety of ways, including traffic monitoring, privacy violations, physical threats, and so on. Guarding against a well-coordinated denial of service attack on a wireless sensor network can be practically hard due to probable asymmetry in power and processing restrictions. There are other attacks possible in WSN other than denial of services such as Traffic analysis attacks, Identity-based attacks, Node replication attacks, and Privacy attacks as shown in figure 2.6.

Jamming a node or a group of nodes is a common denial of service attack on wireless sensor networks. In this scenario, jamming is merely the sending of a radio signal that interferes with the sensor network's radio frequencies. A network's jamming can take two forms: continuous jamming and periodic jamming. Jamming the entire network is what continuous jamming entails.

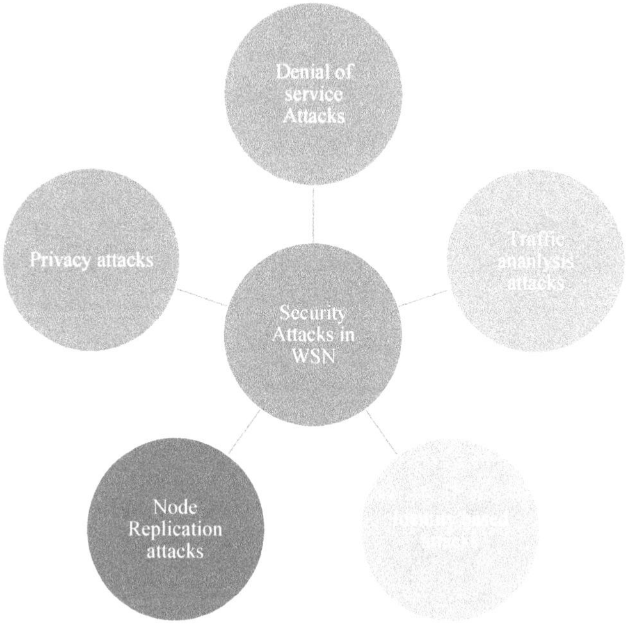

Figure 2.6: Security attacks in WSN

There is no way to send or receive messages. If the jamming is simply periodic, nodes can send and receive messages regularly, but not consistently. Sybil attack is a common type of Identity-based attack, where a malicious or intruder node makes multiple identities illegally and affects the data aggregation, routing algorithms, and fair resource allocation. The Sybil attack, for example, could use numerous identities to produce additional "votes" in a sensor network voting method. Similarly, the Sybil attack on the routing protocol relies on a malicious node impersonating numerous nodes and thereby directing multiple routing paths through a single defective node.

In a traffic analysis attack, the attacker does not need to distort the real data. The attacker just listens in on network traffic to look for key node locations, routing structures, and even application activity patterns. Traffic analysis is used by attackers to determine the location of the base station. After identifying the base station, the attacker can launch a number of attacks against it, such as jamming and eavesdropping. In a node replication attack, an attacker replicates the node ID of an already existing sensor to add a node to an existing sensor network. A sensor network's performance can be substantially harmed by a node replicated in this way: packets can be garbled or even misrouted. This can result in a network disconnect, incorrect sensor readings, and other issues.

The fundamental privacy issue in sensor networks is that using direct site surveillance an adversary can acquire a lot of data from sensor networks. Sensor networks exacerbate the privacy issue by making massive amounts of data easily accessible via remote access. As a result, opponents are not required to be physically present to sustain surveillance. Eavesdropping, monitoring, camouflage, and traffic analysis are common types of privacy attacks in sensor networks. Sensor networks are commonly used in harsh outdoor situations. The small form size of the sensors, along with the unattended and scattered nature of their deployment in such contexts, makes them very vulnerable to physical attacks, such as threats from physical node destruction. Physical attacks, unlike many of the other attacks outlined above, permanently destroy sensors, resulting in irrevocable losses.

The resource-constrained nature of WSN poses a significant security concern. The WSN needs to be protected against different types of attacks. The processing power, battery life, and memory of the WSNs are all limited. To provide a full security system, energy-efficient security measures must be integrated into every component. WSNs must meet several characteristics, including low processing power, limited memory, and the inability to be truly detected, all of which make information security difficult. Cryptography is a common method for securing data in sensor networks. Cryptography can be used to provide authenticity, confidentiality, and integrity in wireless sensor networks. It is critical to choose the right cryptographic algorithm to suit the requirements of WSNs. Processing time, power consumption, code size, and data size are all characteristics used to evaluate cryptographic algorithms. Cryptographic algorithms employed in WSNs should be evaluated based on code size, data size, processing time, and power consumption, as well as the limits of sensor nodes. Due to the computational and memory limitations of sensor nodes, typical cryptography algorithms cannot be easily ported to WSNs. As a result, to meet the aforementioned security criteria, existing approaches must be adapted or new techniques must be invented. We can divide them into two categories based on known cryptography techniques as shown in figure 2.7.

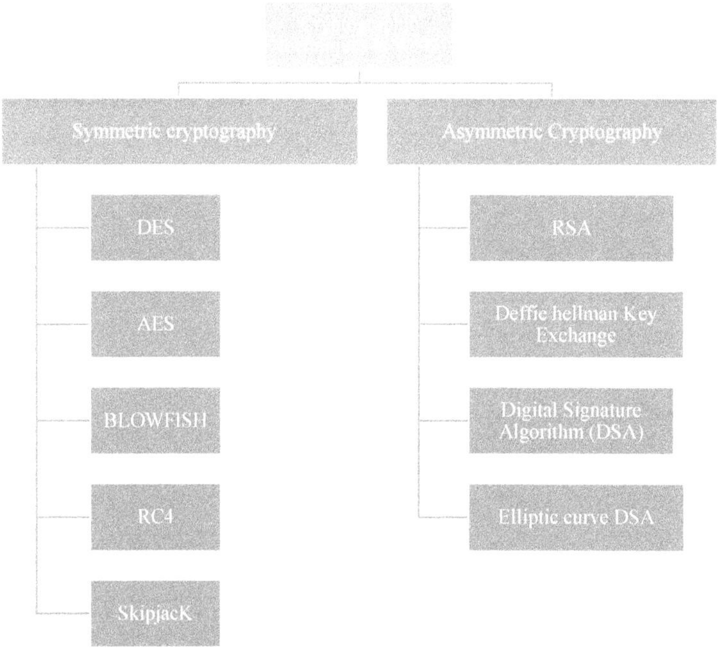

Figure 2.7: Cryptographic algorithms in WSN

cryptographic techniques and symmetric cryptographic techniques are two types of cryptographic techniques [93][97-100].

- **Asymmetric Cryptography**: This technique of cryptography uses two keys for encryption and decryption. The first key known as private key is used to encrypt and sign data in asymmetric cryptography, while a public key is used to decrypt and verify it. The private key must be kept private, whereas the public key can be shared freely. Public-key cryptography, or PKC, is another name for asymmetric cryptography. Public-key encryption is resource expensive and thus regarded infeasible un WSN's hardware because most systems are built on huge integer arithmetic. Due to code complexity, data size, processing time, and power consumption, the employment of public-key method approaches like the Diffie-Hellman key agreement protocol or RSA signatures in WSNs are undesirable.

- **Symmetric Cryptography**: A single shared key is utilized for both encryption and decryption between the two communication nodes in symmetric cryptographic systems. This shared key has to be kept secret, which might be challenging in the open environment of WSNs. Most security solutions for WSN use only symmetric cryptography because they require less power and can be easily implemented on less hardware. The two types of symmetric ciphers used are block ciphers that work on blocks of a certain length and stream ciphers that work bitwise on the data. The term "steam cipher" refers to a block cipher with a block length of 1 bit. AES, DES, IDEA, Blowfish, RC4, RC5, and skipjack are only a few of the most widely used cryptographic algorithms.

Our research begins with a review of recent advances in cryptography techniques for sensor networks. For securing information communicated in WSN, symmetric cryptographic algorithms such as DES (Data Encryption Standard), AES (Advanced Encryption Standard), RC5 (Rivest Cipher), and Blowfish are available.

The authors of [64] compared the energy costs and calculation times of public and private key cryptography algorithms on wireless sensor networks and found that public key is very expensive in terms of energy and computation. In terms of cost, speed, and energy, symmetric or private key cryptography outperforms asymmetric or public-key encryption.

In [65, 66, 67], researchers compared the performance of symmetric models including DES, Triple-DES, Blowfish, and AES in the context of wireless sensor networks. Memory needs, energy usage, CPU clock cycles, and CPU process time are the performance metrics to compare. The power consumption of the CPU is reflected in the CPU clock cycles, according to these papers. A modest quantity of energy is consumed by each CPU cycle. Blowfish is faster than AES and 3DES, according to these papers, but it requires a lot of memory, thus it can't be used in smart cards. In terms of energy usage and throughput, the blowfish outperforms triple-DES and AES. Because the key generation procedure for Blowfish is lengthy, subkeys must be computed ahead of time. When various factors such as data type, data density, data size, and key size are considered, AES outperforms 3DES and blowfish.

Another study [68] proposed that AES S-boxes may be improved by adopting a key-dependent S-box. The key of the round is utilized to rotate S-box in this paper, and numerous options for picking the value from the key to be used for shifting S-box have been proposed. Researchers in [69,70] recommended various changes to the algorithm's key expansion part to increase security and reduce time without hurting the algorithm's efficiency.

The authors of [71] propose a parallel AES implementation on a multiprocessor platform. For round parallelization and pipelining, the design combines Add Round Key and mix Column steps. The proposed system is appropriate for real-time traffic and scalable across large networks. Another study [72] shows how to improve key expansion by mapping 16 AES algorithm implementations with offline and online key expansion on a multi-core system.

A hardware implementation of S-box substitution is presented in a research study [73] to increase the overall speed of S-box replacement. To accomplish quick data encryption, another study [74] uses several threads to encrypt multiple plaintexts concurrently. The paper research [75] enhances the performance of the AES algorithm by using several threads on a multicore computer. Much of the work in the subject of wireless sensor data encryption is centered on hardware-level approaches and strategies for increasing the AES algorithm's performance.

Multithreading has been employed in a multicore platform for parallel encryption of several plaintexts at the software level. Using several threads, on the other hand, does not minimize the time it takes to encrypt a single plaintext, particularly the S-box replacement component. Additionally, when one thread uses the S-box, the other thread must wait.

In [76], the authors describe power-adaptive information encryption for energy-efficient and secure communication in solar-powered WSNs. The research provides an energy-safety level management technique that maximizes the usage of gathered energy while improving encryption and energy efficiency. When the sensor node's residual energy is high, public-key encryption techniques like elliptic curve cryptography (ECC) are employed, and when the node's residual energy is low, symmetric key encryption techniques like AES are used.

The study researcher[77] proposes a collection of security building pieces that are tailored to resource-constrained and wireless communication contexts. Two protected building blocks make up a security protocol for sensor networks (SPINS): The initial building block incorporates the following fundamental basic safety primitives: data security, data authentication, and data freshness; for data encryption, AES is employed. The second component is a contemporary protocol that enables authenticated broadcasting in high-resource scenarios.

Another study [78] proposes the RB-OOIBE (Receiver-Bounded Online / Offline Identity-Based Encryption) identity-based encryption system for WSN applications. This divides the encryption process into two halves, one offline and one online. The offline part performs both the costly computations and the plaintext message without knowing the receiver's identity. On the online level, only light computations such as modular operation and symmetric key encryption, as well as the receiver identification and plaintext message, are required.

Using the notion of addition chains (AC), research in [79] suggests an improvement in RSA and ECC cryptographic algorithms for android and windows emulators. Particle swarm optimization techniques is used to create the AC. The proposed method shortens the time it takes to decrypt and encrypt data, lowering WSN power consumption.

Using reversible logic gates, the authors of [80] introduced a revolutionary version of the AES cryptographic algorithm utilized in WSN. These reversible logic gates are ideal for developing quantum computers since they use no power. The new AES design provided here lowers the power consumption of WSNs while simultaneously making them less sensitive to power analysis attacks.

In [81], researchers developed a small-area, co-processor-based version of the AES encryption algorithm for WSN. To achieve a small and low-cost design, field arithmetic sharing and reuse technology were used for circuit impulsion. In addition, the study examines the WSN's security procedures.

Another study [82] employs a hybrid encryption approach to encrypt and decrypt highly sensitive biomedical data in wireless body area networks. For encryption and decryption, the authors used two encryption techniques in parallel: Elliptic curve cryptography (ECC) and AES. Both encryption techniques encrypt with the same key. Half of the data is encrypted by each algorithm.

AES is a fast encryption technique that may be utilized across multiple platforms, including embedded devices. AES is quick in both hardware and software, and it's simple to set up. For remote sensing systems, AES is the most well-known and widely used symmetric-key encryption computation. AES is simple to implement in both software and hardware on 8-bit embedded microprocessors. In any case, the AES calculation has some drawbacks, such as the S-box query table being a time-consuming procedure. Each round requires the substitution of 16 bytes of an input data matrix.

2.5 RESEARCH GAPS, RESEARCH OBJECTIVES, AND RESEARCH CONTRIBUTIONS

Research Gaps (RG) - Based upon the literature survey, we identified the following major research gaps (RG) from the literature defined as follows:

RG1: The real-world applications often require the deployment of a high-density sensor network. Such networks with high-density clusters face the problems of energy holes. Moreover, with a large number of nodes, such clusters are not suitable for data aggregation, resulting in data loss and delays. Resultantly, data freshness could not be maintained.

RG2: The existing work in WSN mostly refers to data aggregation with statistical techniques, like average, maximum, k-means, etc. Swarm Intelligence based techniques are mainly used for routing, clustering, and tree-based aggregation. The prevailing research is found to be significantly deficient in applying swarm intelligence for better performance in data aggregation such as execution time and quantization error.

RG3: In the context of time-series data prediction for sensor networks, existing models mainly make use of ARIMA, SVM, KNN, and Linear Regression (LR) for the prediction process. Without making any real-time alterations to the real data, all of these approaches and models use training data to build a model and then test data to predict future values. Resultantly, the prediction error and frequency of data transmissions become high, thereby consuming the energy of the battery-operated sensor nodes.

RG4: The existing work on data security in sensor networks uses symmetric cryptographic algorithms such as AES, DES, RC5, Blowfish, etc. The AES, though most widely used, is slow as compared to other algorithms due to its time-consuming byte substitution process. As a result, energy consumption also becomes high.

Research Objectives (RO) - are identified as a problem to solve the research gaps identified in the literature discussed in the previous section, and hence are summarized as follows:

RO1: To address the problem of energy holes in sensor networks by reducing the size of large clusters, thereby minimizing transmission delay and preventing data loss in cluster-based operations, like data aggregation, etc.

RO2: To explore swarm intelligence-based data aggregation techniques for reducing the execution time and error involved in the aggregation process of sensed data.

RO3: To reduce the prediction error and number of transmissions from sensor node to cluster head in time-series based data prediction in a sensor network to improve the lifetime of the sensor network.

RO4: To improve the speed of the AES encryption algorithm and reduce the power consumed during encryption and decryption for improving the functional lifetime of the sensor network.

Research Contributions (RC) - are identified as a solution to fulfil the research objectives described in the previous section, and are summarized as follows:

RC1: Designed a recursive density based hierarchical data-oriented clustering algorithm for Gaussian distributed sensor network, for addressing the problem of energy holes, and create discrete small clusters within high-density clusters using a hierarchical approach to support rapid data aggregation, thus preserving the freshness of sensed data.

RC2: Proposed a PSO-based Sensor Network Aggregation Protocol (PSO-SNAP), which uses a novel fitness function to perform data aggregation with minimum quantization error and reduced execution time than existing approaches.

RC3: Designed an On-balance-volume based Data Prediction (ODP) model for sensor networks that can perform stepwise temperature prediction along with a real-time adjustment by the real-world data stream, thereby improving prediction accuracy with the relatively fewer number of data transmission from sensor node to cluster head. Also, develop an approach for handling errors in case the predicted value exceeds the pre-determined data tolerance limit.

RC4: Proposed energy efficient and faster version of the AES encryption algorithm for the sensor network and compare its performance with existing benchmark algorithms. The research focus is to apply the concept of multithreading for parallel programming support, to minimize the overall energy consumption.

CHAPTER 3

DATA CLUSTERING

This chapter describes the first research contribution (data clustering) in wireless sensor networks. It describes the methodology and algorithm of the proposed recursive density based hierarchical clustering (RDHC) model. The proposed model has been proven to be effective in solving the problem of energy holes in WSN and creating discrete and balanced clusters.

3.1 OVERVIEW

In sensor networks, specialized energy-aware data gathering algorithms with high scalability and network longevity are required. In WSN, clustering is employed to overcome the issue of energy holes. Data aggregation is not ideal for clusters with a large number of nodes, resulting in data loss and delays. Soft computing technologies are increasingly being used in the development of real-time decision-making solutions. Probabilistic modeling is one of the most important pillars of soft computing since it allows you to propose solutions based on statistical distributions. The proposed work in our research contribution is centered on a probabilistic technique to building recursive density-based clustering of uniformly Gaussian distributed sensors. The automatic radii computation framework is built with probabilistic cluster size identification based on the geo-positioning of the sensor nodes. Furthermore, real-time outlier prediction is used to compare the performance of our proposed model to that of existing density-based methods. As a result, our novel research considers multiple criteria for selecting whether sensor nodes belong to the proper cluster based on sensor density distribution.

3.1.1 Current state-of-art methods

The current state-of-art method for density-based clustering includes the Data density-based clustering algorithm DDC and DDCAR. The DDC algorithm creates clusters depending on the geographic density of data points. DDC does not require the number of clusters as an input like DBSCAN. It requires the user to enter an initial radius. The cluster head is determined in the first step, and then the starting radius is used to include data points in the cluster. The cluster is refined and the cluster radii are updated in the second step. The user input serves as a restraint. In DDCAR, an enhancement to the DDC method has been proposed to automatically determine initial radii.

DDCAR does not drive small clusters into large clusters, resulting in a huge number of small clusters. As a result, DDCAR enables more precise grouping. The DDCAR algorithm does not require any human input in the form of cluster number, beginning radii, or knowledge of data point density. DDCAR only works with Euclidean distances. AGDStream, MDStream, HDDStream, DCStream, are other density-based data stream clustering algorithms. These techniques start with grid-based clustering and then find dense and sparse grids by looking at the density values associated with each data point. The clusters produced by these algorithms are pure and accurate with memory and time being the two significant limitations in these algorithms.

3.2 PROPOSED RECURSIVE DENSITY BASED HIERARCHICAL CLUSTERING METHODOLOGY

In sensor networks, a scenario-specific approach for density-based hierarchical clustering has been presented. A high-density sensor network is employed for the project, with the base station positioned in the center for improved coverage and additional nodes performing data sampling, transmission, and relaying. The sensor network's useful lifetime is limited in such networks because the nodes surrounding the base station are quickly exhausted due to the high load. Energy holes are created as a result of this. The ideal technique to depict such networks is with Gaussian distributed sensor networks. For simulation, Gaussian distributed datasets are utilized because they can easily depict high-density sensor networks. To address the aforementioned issues, we must divide the large-scale, high-density one-cloud of sensor nodes into small clusters, each with its cluster head. This procedure can be used recursively to break down large clusters into smaller clusters, resulting in hierarchical clusters. This will make data collecting and management easier, and the network's performance will improve as a result. Due to the spatial layout of density distributed sensor nodes, the research project is centered on recognizing inherently present clusters.

3.2.1 Overview of DDC and DDCAR algorithms

The DDC technique can be used to do clustering-based data density on big datasets. The DDC algorithm takes cluster radii as input from the user and clusters sensor nodes in a sensor network using a recursive density estimation technique. The DDC algorithm is not completely self-contained because it requires the user to provide initial radii. The smallest cluster size is two. The

DDC technique has been revised and extended in DDCAR to automatically discover the appropriate initial radii value by applying data density calculations to the input data; the remainder of DDCAR's methodology is identical to the DDC algorithm. The DDCAR additionally accepts an extra argument, c, which specifies the minimum cluster size. Because 'c' is optional and not part of the core algorithm, the DDCAR creates a cluster of all the points in the input dataset. The DDCAR algorithm's steps are listed below:

1. Load the input global data set
2. Estimate the initial radii for each axis
3. Find the sample density of each point and calculate the global mean and scalar product of all the data points.
4. The highest density sample is assigned as cluster center, and all the points that lie within the initial cluster radii (as calculated in step 2) from the cluster center are assigned to one cluster.
5. For the cluster formed in step 4, find the local mean and scalar product and density of each point in the cluster.
6. Find the updated cluster center and assign all the points that lie within cluster radii to the updated cluster.
7. The initial cluster radii are updated
8. If the points which are not part of any cluster are greater than minimum cluster size 'c', then go to step 3 again.

3.2.2 Proposed RDHC Model Overview

To create small and hierarchical clusters in a Gaussian distributed sensor network, the suggested methodology uses the Recursive Density based Hierarchical Clustering (RDHC) technique. According to related work on density-based clustering approaches, DDCAR is a fully automated and efficient data clustering methodology that does not require any human input, unlike other density-based techniques. The suggested technique employs a recursive application of a modified DDCAR clustering algorithm to create hierarchical clusters. To keep a check on the recursive approach, the proposed solution uses a threshold variable 't'. The threshold value is a predetermined network parameter that specifies the recursive approach's base case. The t-value also serves as a minimum cluster size. Outliers or noise is detected using the threshold value. The program will recursively find hierarchical clusters until the dataset size exceeds t. The time spent collecting and aggregating data in small clusters will be reduced, reducing transmission delay and maintaining data freshness. The proposed algorithm's highlights are as follows:

- By installing more sensors near the base station or cluster head, the energy hole problem is addressed by density-based clustering.
- By using recursive clustering to create clusters inside clusters, balanced clusters are generated.
- Within the cluster, the average transmission distance between nodes and cluster heads is lowered.
- The risk of a collision is lessened as traffic is reduced.
- Packet transmission time is cut in half since fewer retransmissions are required.
- Data aggregation in the network could be done quickly, saving time and ensuring data freshness.

The proposed RDHC algorithm is an improvement in the existing density-based clustering algorithm (DDCAR):

- It accepts non-Euclidean distance measures, such as standard Euclidean distance.
- Hierarchical clustering is supported, which aids data aggregation in large clusters.
- Outliers are being removed from clusters to make them more precise and apparent.
- In contrast to DDCAR, no input data normalization is performed.

3.2.3 Proposed RDHC Algorithmic Framework

The Recursive Density-based Hierarchical Clustering (RDHC) technique we propose uses an automatic method for estimating the cluster's initial radius r from the input dataset. The formulae that were utilized to create the clusters and determine the initial radius are listed below. The N represents the size of the dataset used for making cluster and xi denotes the ith sample. Table 3.1 lists the many symbols and assumptions utilized in the RDHC clustering algorithm.

Table 3.1: Symbols and assumptions used in RDHC data clustering algorithm

S.no	Symbol	Description
1	N	Size of data set
2	x_i	The ith data sample
3	t	The threshold value and minimum cluster size
4	μ_o	The Global mean (mean of all the samples)
5	X_O	Global Scalar product
6	d_i	distance between sample i and mean μ_o
7	D_i	The density of each sample
8	r_j	The radius of cluster j
9	$\bar{\delta}$	Mean density change
10	m_i	Moving average density change
11	δ_i	Local density change
12	r_o	Initial radius
13	c	Cluster center
14	n	density changes used for smoothing
15	k	No. of clusters formed
16	μ_j	the local mean of cluster j

The mathematical equations used in the proposed RDHC algorithm are mentioned below:

The global mean is denoted by μ_o is the average of all the data samples considered.

$$\mu_{o}=\frac{1}{N}\sum_{i-1}^{N} x_i \tag{3.1}$$

The scalar product X_o is used to calculate the density of each sample from the dataset.

$$X_{o=}\frac{1}{N}\sum_{i-1}^{N} x_i^2 \qquad (3.2)$$

The distance metric d_i used to find the distance between two data points can use the following distances. (a) The Euclidean distance –is the line distance between a sample i and mean μ_o.

(b) Standardized euclidean distance – is used to balance the contributions of different variables thus standardization is done by using $s_i = \frac{x_i-\mu_o}{\sigma}$ where σ is the standard deviation.

The density of each sample of the dataset D_i is set using the values of mean μ_o, scalar product X_o, and distance metric d_i, calculated in the above equations. The Euclidean norm has been used in the equation (3.3). The Euclidean distance of a vector from the origin is a norm known as the Euclidean norm, which can also be defined as the square root of a vector's inner product with itself. The Euclidean distance has been used to find the distance of the data samples from the mean.

$$D_i = \frac{1}{1 + d_i^2 + X_o - \|\mu_0\|^2} \qquad (3.3)$$

The radius of cluster 'j' in each dimension 'k' denoted by r_{jk} is modified using the values of the sample and mean in that dimension

$$r_{jk} = \max(\|x_{jk} - \mu_{jk}\|) \qquad (3.4)$$

The Mean Density Change $\bar{\delta}$ is calculated as follows:

$$\bar{\delta} = \frac{1}{N}\sum_{n=2}^{N} (D_n - D_{n-1}) \qquad (3.5)$$

Moving average density change m_i is calculated to smooth the densities

$$m_i = \frac{1}{n}\sum_{i-n}^{i} (D_i - D_{i-1}) \qquad (3.6)$$

Local Density change δ_i for each data is calculated, as follows

$$\delta_i = |m_i - m_{i-1}| \qquad (3.7)$$

The algorithmic design for the proposed recursive approach is illustrated in algorithms 3.1, 3.2 and 3.3.

Algorithm 3.1: Recursive_Density_Hierarchical_Clustering (Dataset, N, t)

Input: Dataset, Size of Dataset (N), Minimum Cluster Size Threshold t

Procedure:

1. if ($N < t$) Then
2. Print "Clustering Process Complete"
3. return
4. else
5. [Clusters, k] = Make_RDHC_Clusters(Data, N, t)
6. Remove Outlier Clusters & Update k
7. for i = 1 To k
8. Call Recursive_Density_Hierarchical_Clustering(Clusters(I), Size(Clusters(i)), t)
9. end-for
10. end-if

Output: k Clusters

Algorithm 3.2: Make_RDHC_Clusters (Data, N, t)

Input: Dataset, Size of Dataset (N), Minimum Cluster Size Threshold t

Procedure:

1. r_o = Calculate_Initial_Radius (dataset, N)
2. Calculate global mean $\mu_{o}=\frac{1}{N}\sum_{i=1}^{N} x_i$
3. Calculate the global scalar product $X_{o}=\frac{1}{N}\sum_{i=1}^{N} x_i^2$
4. Calculate the density of each sample $D_i = \frac{1}{1+d_i^2+X_o-\|\mu_o\|^2}$
5. Cluster center $c = max(D_i)$ sample
6. All points within the initial radii r_o of the cluster center is assigned to cluster
7. All points having distance > 3σ from cluster center are returned to global dataset N.
8. Find local mean μ_j, X_o, D_i of each point i included in cluster j using steps 2, 3, and 4.
9. Move cluster center $c = max(D_i)$
10. All points within the initial radii r_o of updated cluster center are assigned to cluster
11. All points that have a distance > 3σ from the cluster center are returned to global dataset N.
12. Update the value of radii $r_j = \max(\|x_j - \mu_j\|)$
13. If the number of samples is not clustered > t then go to step 2
14. end

Output: k clusters with cluster numbers are formed

Algorithm 3.3: Calculate_Initial_radius(Dataset, N)

Input: Dataset, Size of Dataset (N)

Procedure: Calculate initial radii using the following steps:

1. Calculate global mean $\mu_{o=}\frac{1}{N}\sum_{i=1}^{N} x_i$
2. Calculate global scalar product $X_{o=}\frac{1}{N}\sum_{i=1}^{N} x_i^2$
3. Calculate density of each sample $D_i = \frac{1}{1+d_i^2+X_o-\|\mu_o\|^2}$
4. Sort D_i in descending order
5. Calculate mean density change $\bar{\delta} = \frac{1}{N}\sum_{n=2}^{N} D_n - D_{n-1}$
6. for each sample i,
7. find moving density change $m_i = \frac{1}{N}\sum_{i-N}^{i} D_i - D_{i-1}$
8. end-for
9. for each sample i,
10. find local density change $\delta_i = |m_i - m_{i-1}|$
11. end-for
12. Find where first δ_i>$\bar{\delta}$ and use this data sample as initial radii r_o
13. End

Output: Initial Radius r_o

3.3 EXPERIMENTATION RESULTS AND ANALYSIS

For sensor nodes, we use Gaussian distributed datasets in our experiments. There are five clouds of data in these datasets, each with random samples. There are 3000 sensor nodes in total, grouped in high-density cloud formations. MATLAB is used to implement the algorithm. MATLAB is a multi - paradigm numerical programming environment for computing. MATLAB has interactive interface that is user-friendly that provides integrated platform for calculation, programing, and visualization, with questions and answers presented in standard format. The main program is algorithm 3.1, which is also the first program that is called. Algorithm 3.1 is a recursive program for recursive clustering of an input data set, which calls Algorithm 3.2 repeatedly until the number of nodes left for clustering is more than 't' (threshold on the minimum cluster size). The extended DDCAR code, Algorithm 3.2, uses standardized Euclidean distance and removes outliers at each iteration. If the number of nodes in a cluster exceeds 't,' a recursive call is made to further divide that large cluster into small clusters. Algorithm 3.2 is a modified DDCAR algorithm that uses a distance metric other than Euclidean, such as standardized Euclidean, and does not normalize the input data.

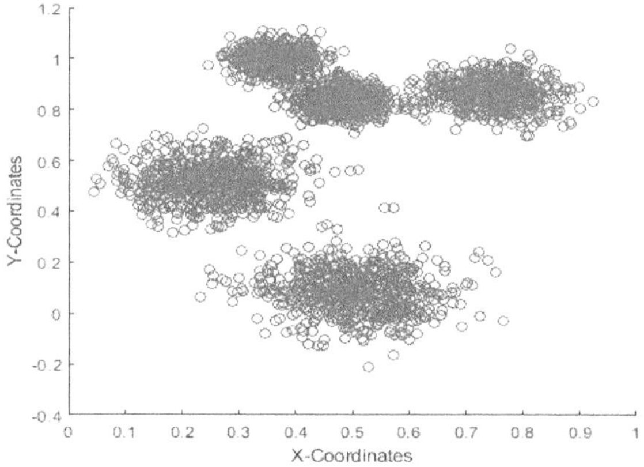

Figure 3.1 : Original gaussian distributed sensor dataset

The program is evaluated using a Gaussian dataset with 3000 sensor nodes grouped in dense clouds and a threshold of t=0.5 of the original dataset's nodes. The threshold value is subject to change. Noise is defined as clusters with less than t samples. The plot of the original Gaussian distributed dataset is shown in Figure 3.1.

3.3.1 Proposed RDHC algorithm outcomes

Figure 3.2 depicts the first layer of clustering on the dataset using the original algorithm, revealing a total of 10 clusters. Figure 3.3 demonstrates the first layer of clustering using the suggested RDHC algorithm on the original dataset, resulting in a total of 7 clusters. When comparing the two figures, it is clear that the proposed method produces more precise and concrete clusters than the original technique. Second, as shown in figure 3.4, the suggested approach also removes noisy data points depending on the value of the threshold and identifies them as outliers, which was not done in the original algorithm. At layer 1 clustering, the suggested approach removes 17 nodes, which is the total number of outliers removed. After removing the outliers, the total number of clusters produced is 3.5, which is adequate given the node layout in the dataset.

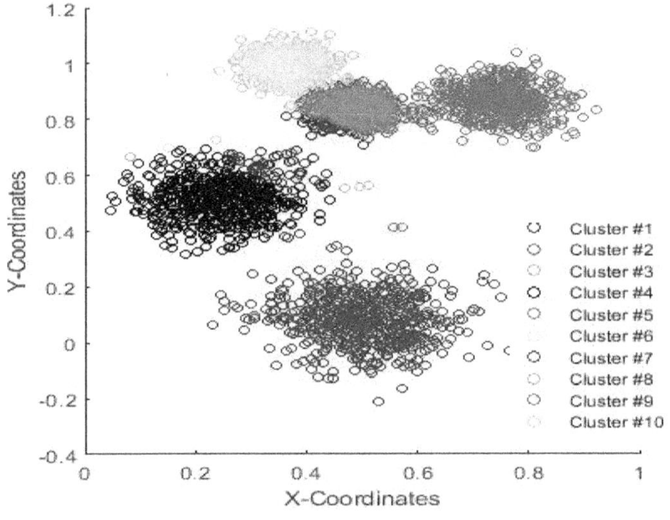

Figure 3.2: Layer 1 clustering of dataset using original algorithm

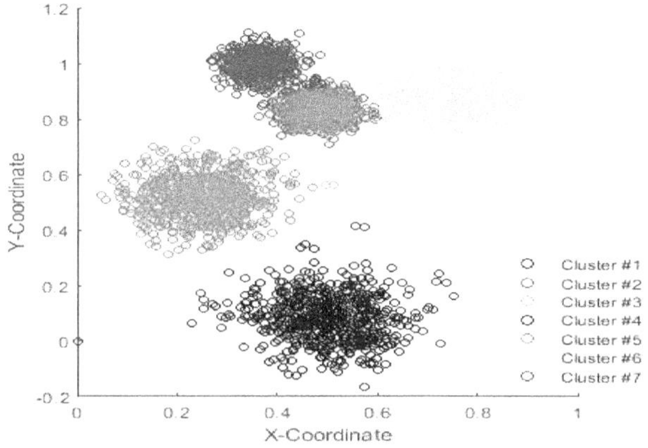

Figure 3.3: Layer 1 clustering of dataset using propsoed RDHC algorithm

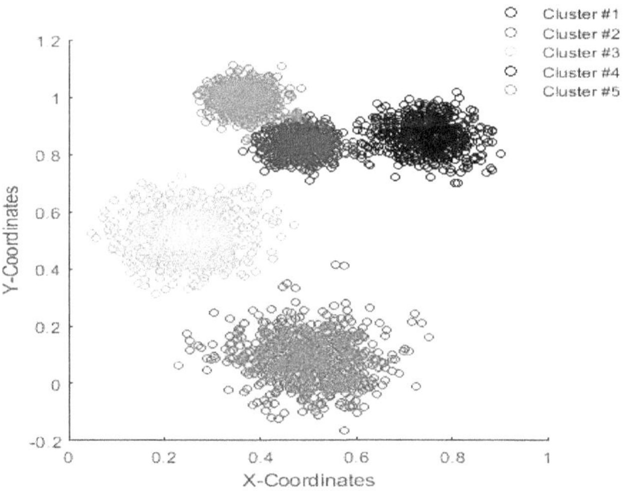

Figure 3.4: Layer 1 clustering of dataset after removing outliers from figure-3.3

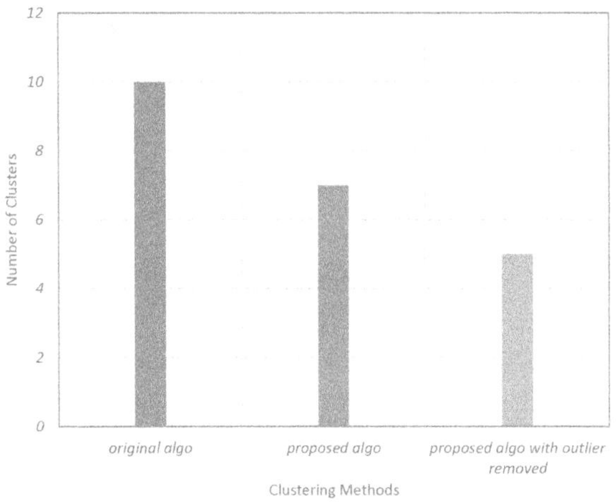

Figure 3.5: Different clustering approaches and the numbers of clusters

In addition, the proposed method employs a recursive clustering strategy to create sub-clusters inside large clusters, which aids in data processing, aggregation, and prediction in large sensor networks. Figure 3.5 depicts a graph comparing the number of groups created by various clustering methods. The graph demonstrates that the proposed technique produces more precise and concrete clusters than the previous algorithm. In addition, as illustrated in the graph, the proposed technique excludes clusters with a size smaller than the threshold and labels those nodes as outliers. Now, using the proposed algorithm, layer -2 clustering is applied to the clusters created in figure 3.4 to produce figures 3.6(a) to 3.6(e).

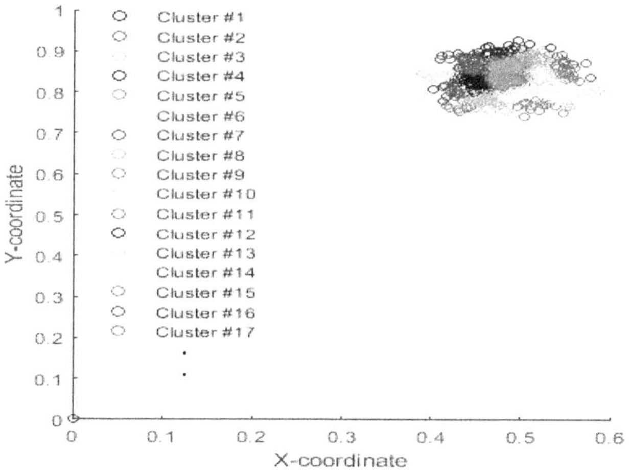

Figure 3.6(a) : Layer 2 clustering on cluster #1 of figure 3.4

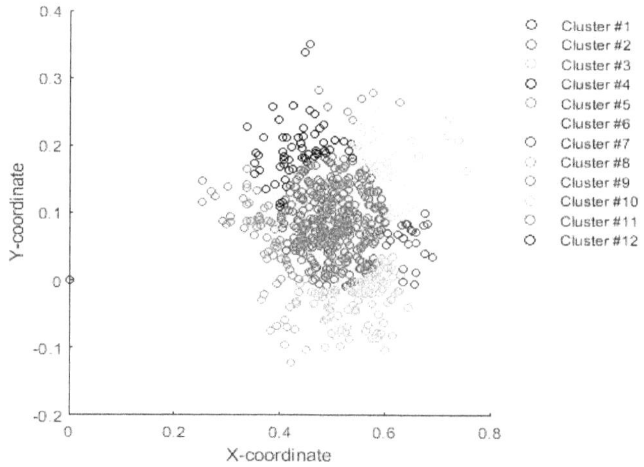

Figure 3.6(b) : Layer 2 clustering on cluster #2 of figure 3.4

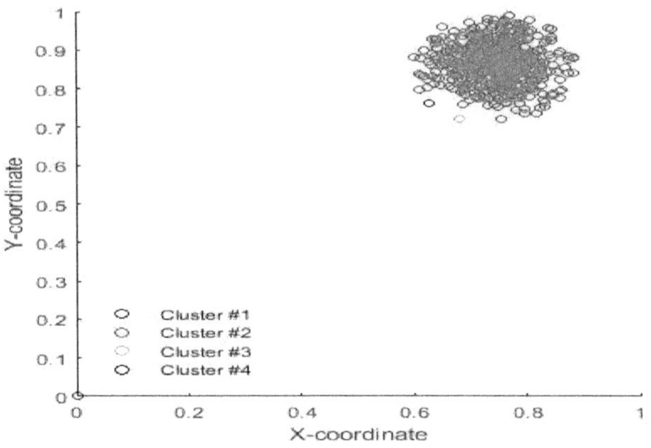

Figure 3.6(c) : Layer 2 clustering on cluster #3 of figure 3.4

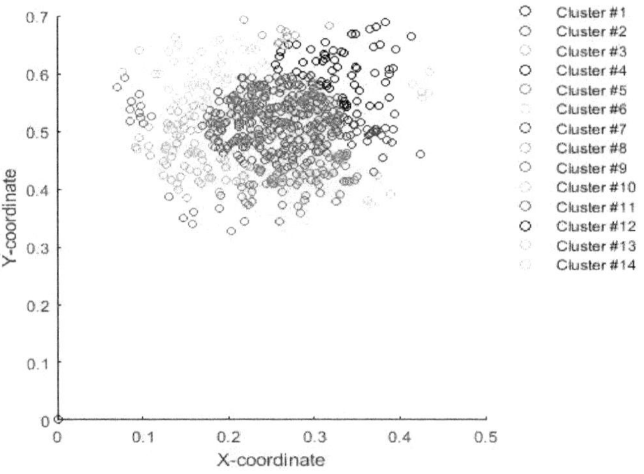

Figure 3.6(d) : Layer 2 clustering on cluster #4 of figure 3.4

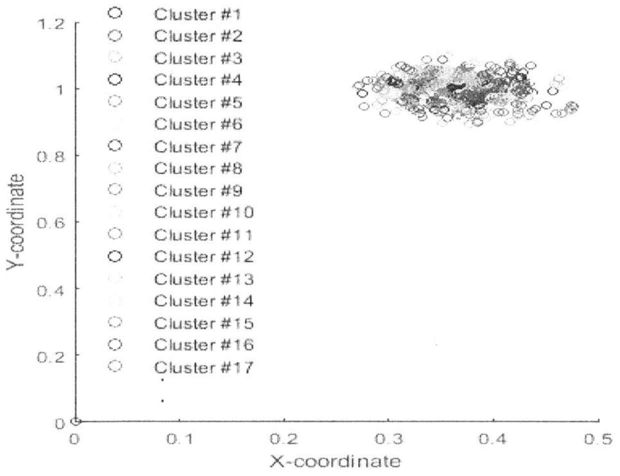

Figure 3.6(e) : Layer 2 clustering on cluster #5 of figure 3.4

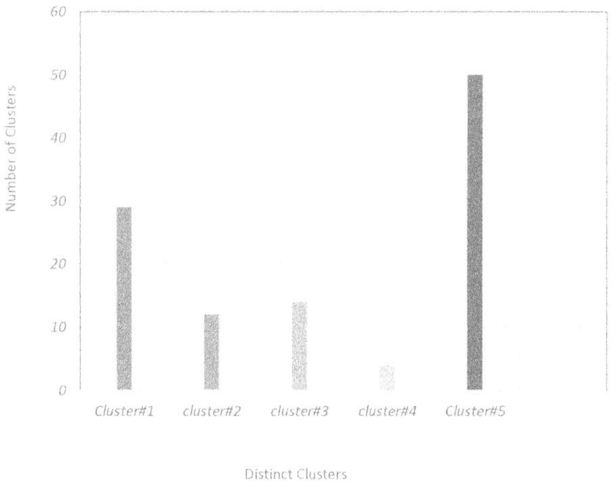

Figure 3.6(f) : Sub clusters formed after Layer 2 clustering in each of main cluster of figure 3.4

The graph of the number of sub-clusters created in the clusters of layer 1 of figure 3.4 is shown in figure 3.6(f). The graph shows that the number of clusters created in layer 2 clustering varies based on the number of clusters and the arrangement of nodes in each cluster. Cluster #5 has the most sub-clusters, with over 40 clusters, many of which are outliers. Outliers are removed from figures 3.6(a) to 3.6(e) using the suggested technique, and the corrected figures are shown in figures 3.7(a) to 3.7 (e). Figure 3.7(e) shows that only four clusters are genuine, while the remainder (about 40) were outliers, depending on the threshold value. Outliers are discovered and deleted based on the threshold value, which changes from cluster to cluster. If the threshold value is changed from 0.5 percent, the outliers will be affected as well. Figure 3.8 shows the total number of outliers removed from each sub-cluster produced in layer 2 of the figures 3.6(a) to 3.6(e).

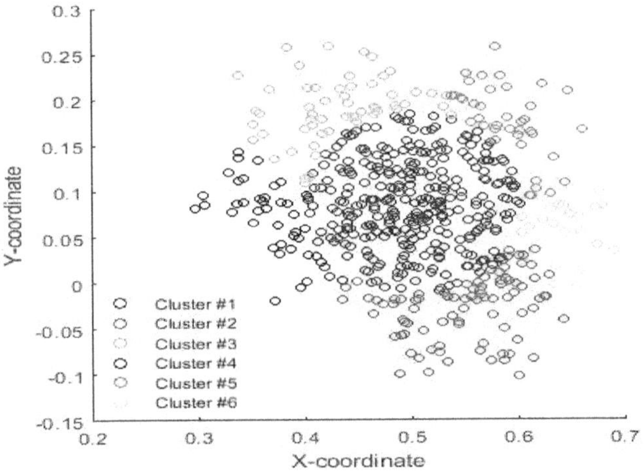

Figure 3.7(a): Clusters after outlier removal from figure 3.6(a)

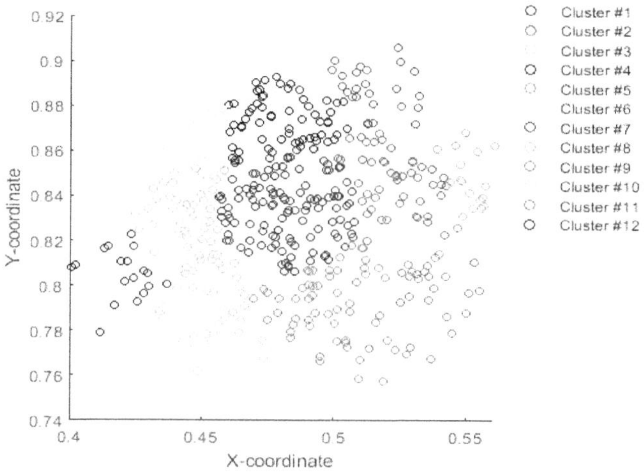

Figure 3.7(b): Clusters after outlier removal from figure 3.6(b)

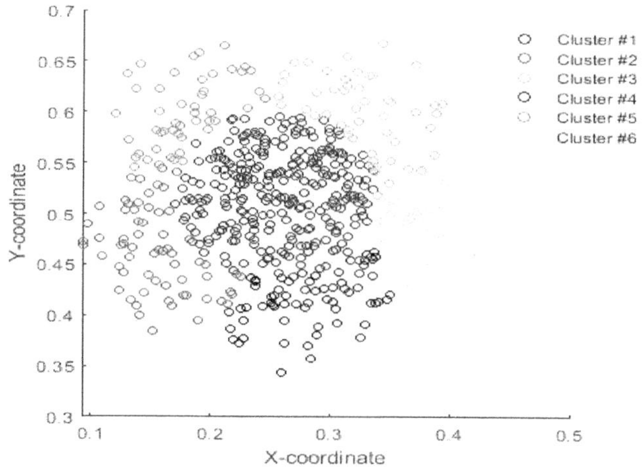

Figure 3.7(c): Clusters after outlier removal from figure 3.6(c)

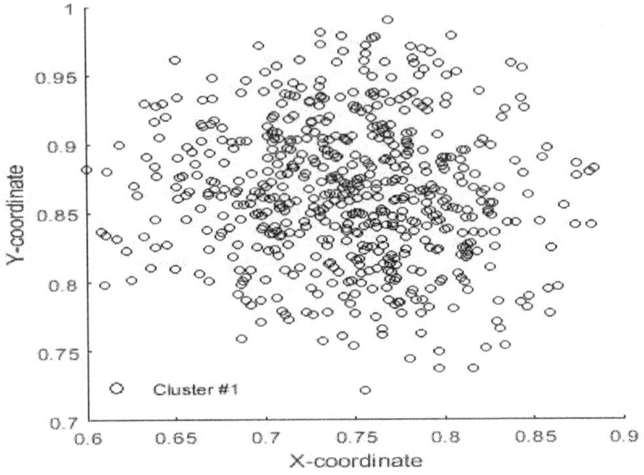

Figure 3.7(d): Clusters after outlier removal from figure 3.6(d)

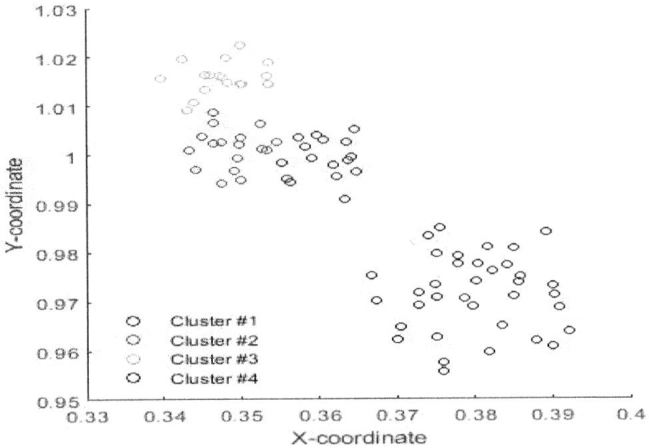

Figure 3.7(e): Clusters after outlier removal from figure 3.6(e)

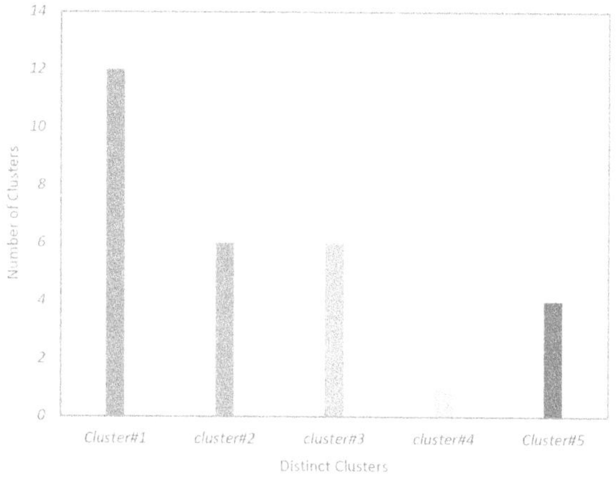

Figure 3.7(f) : Sub clusters formed after removing outliers from each of main cluster of figure 3.4

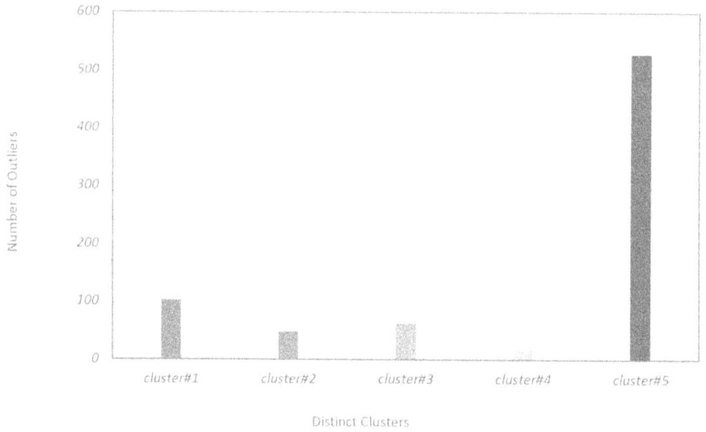

Figure 3.8: Total number of outliers removed

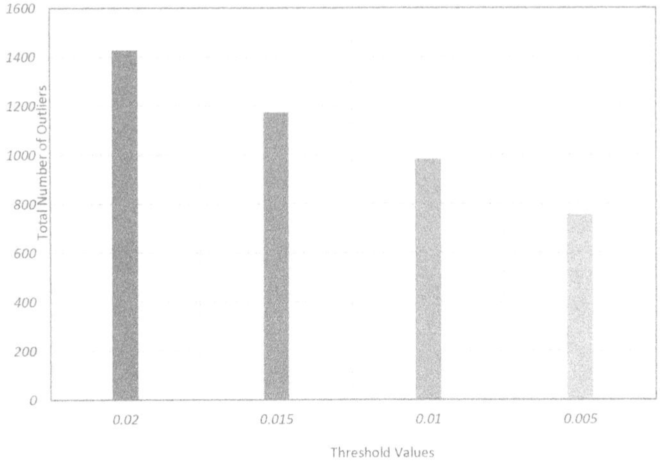

Figure 3.9: Total number of outliers removed in Layer 2 clustering based on different values of threshold

The detection of outliers is based on the threshold value. Figure 3.9 shows that as the threshold value increases from 0.5 percent to 2 percent with a step size of 0.5 percent, more outliers are removed. In the research, we used a threshold value of 0.5 percent for experimentation.

3.4 SUMMARY

Due to the sensors' functionality of reporting data to the base station located at the center of a Gaussian distributed network, wireless sensor networks face the energy hole problem. As a result, the number of retransmissions and delays rise, and the data becomes obsolete. This research answers the problem by grouping the sensor network using a soft computing-based probabilistic recurrence method and density-based recursive hierarchical clustering. In comparison to the existing counterpart, our unique recursive process produces better and more accurate clusters. The proposed RDHC clustering algorithm applies recursive methodology and makes better and accurate clusters as compared to the exiting counterpart. It addresses the energy hole problem in sensor networks.

Our proposed RDHC:

- Forms discrete and appropriate clusters
- Removes a limited number of outliers
- Ensures loss of minimum sensor data

This reduces the number of retransmissions and maintains the data freshness. The recursive clustering helps in better data aggregation and data prediction. The proposed technique, which uses a 0.5 percent outlier criterion, identifies different clusters and addresses the energy hole problem, lowering the number of retransmissions.

CHAPTER 4

DATA AGGREGATION

This chapter explains the second research contribution in wireless sensor networks. A lot of power is consumed when the data is transmitted from the sensor node to the base station. As a result, effective data aggregation algorithms are required to reduce energy consumption in sensor networks. This chapter describes the methodology of the proposed particle swarm optimization-based data aggregation algorithm. The proposed data aggregation algorithm has proven to be effective against standard data aggregation algorithms when compared based on quantization error and execution time.

4.1 OVERVIEW

A wireless sensor network (WSN) is made up of a collection of sensor nodes as well as a base station node located near the sensor network. The base station serves as a gateway to the internet and other networks, sending commands to sensor nodes and collecting data from them regularly. Because the sensor network's data is massive and extensively duplicated, data aggregation is used, and only the relevant compound data is sent to the sink. Data aggregation aggregates data to eliminate duplicates and reduce the amount of data sent from the sensor network to the base station. In a WSN, data aggregation enhances bandwidth while lowering power consumption.

The data aggregation process entails gathering raw data from many sensors, applying programming techniques to enhance the data, and then delivering the modified data to end consumers. Data aggregation minimizes the load on sensor nodes, allowing for more efficient handling of data with priority. Data aggregation approaches have a few drawbacks, such as longer processing times and higher system needs. Redundancy, delay, data accuracy, and network longevity are key issues that each data aggregation technique faces. For aggregating data, functions such as minimum, maximum, average, count, and so on are used.

The cluster and group-based approaches outperform the other data aggregation techniques in terms of longevity, accuracy, and dependability. Swarm intelligence (SI) approaches are evolutionary computing techniques based on biologically inspired artificial intelligence that has lately acquired popularity in the scientific community for tackling optimization challenges. Techniques based on swarm intelligence are increasingly being used to solve optimization problems because they provide better convergence to the solution. To solve complicated issues, SI employs the notions of division of labor and self-organization. The Swarm intelligence is based on the behavior of social insects such as fish, birds, ants, bees, and wasps in groups. Scheduling, load balancing, clustering, routing, and optimization are all domains where swarm intelligence techniques are applied. Many algorithms are based on swarm intelligence such as ant colony optimization (ACO). The particle swarm optimization (PSO) technique is based on the behavior of a swarm of birds or a school of fish. We employed PSO to accomplish cluster-based data aggregation in the WSN in this research.

4.1.1 Current state-of-art methods

There are several data aggregation techniques that uses swarm intelligence-based data aggregation techniques. Particle Swarm Optimization (PSO) has been used for data aggregation in sensor network. The number of sensor nodes, average distance, initial energy, and remaining energy are used to construct the PSO fitness function. When compared to ant colony and genetic algorithm optimization strategies, the PSO-based method is found to be superior to the other two in terms of energy consumption and network longevity. PSO has been utilized for data aggregation to deliver the best solutions for three problems: optimal transmission power allocation, determining the best local threshold, and the sensor setup. ACO has been used for In-network data aggregation in WSN. An integrated technique using divide and conquer and enhanced K-means to do data aggregation at sensor node and cluster head level is also used in WSN. The integrated approach not only saves energy but also preserves the data accuracy at the base station.

4.1.2 Highlights of Research Contribution

The following are the primary contributions of our research:

- In the wireless sensor network, swarm intelligence was used to aggregate data.
- A unique fitness function was proposed for a PSO-based sensor network aggregation protocol (PSO-SNAP).

- The suggested PSO-SNAP beat the existing standard PSO method in terms of quantization error and execution time.
- A comparison analysis was conducted using K-means, K-medoid, and simple average across different versions of the proposed PSO-SNAP.

Justification for PSO-based Research w.r.t. other Swarm Intelligence techniques:

Among the other swarm intelligence based approaches such as Ant Colony Optimization (ACO) and Genetic Algorithm, PSO features simple and easy computations (GA). PSO requires minimal parameters for adjustment, and unlike genetic algorithms, it does not require mutation and crossover operators for evolution, thus it can study quickly. ACO is a method of testing that involves making a series of random judgments. ACO is a discrete optimization technique, while PSO is a stochastic optimization technique. The time it takes for ACO to reach convergence is unknown, but PSO does it quickly. PSO outperforms other swarm intelligence-based strategies in terms of performance and convergence. As a result, PSO was chosen as our recommended data aggregation method.

4.2 PROPOSED PSO BASED SENSOR AGGREGATION PROTOCOL

This research is aimed at a two-level clustering-based hierarchical sensor network made up of sensor nodes and grouped into clusters. Each node senses the temperature from the environment and sends it to the head of the cluster after local aggregation. The cluster head gets sensed data from all of the sensor nodes regularly and then perform data aggregation before transmitting the aggregated data to the sink. Both the sensor node and the cluster head can benefit from the proposed algorithm. The weighted sensor network data aggregation protocol based on PSO namely (PSO-SNAP) has been proposed. The K-medoid, K-means, and simple average of the input data are employed with the PSO-SNAP. The PSO algorithm is seeded with an initial centroid using the K-means, K-medoid, and simple average algorithms, and then the PSO algorithm is used to find the particle's best position. The algorithm's goal is to locate the best swarm position with the least amount of quantization error. The proposed algorithm's flow diagram is shown in Figure 4.1.

In the experimental analysis, the results of the three PSO-SNAP approaches using K-means, K-medoid, and simple average are compared and analyzed. The suggested PSO-SNAP method is also compared to a standard PSO-based data aggregation approach in which the quantization error is quantized using Euclidean distance rather than weighted distance. The symbolic notations used in the paper are listed in Table 4.1.

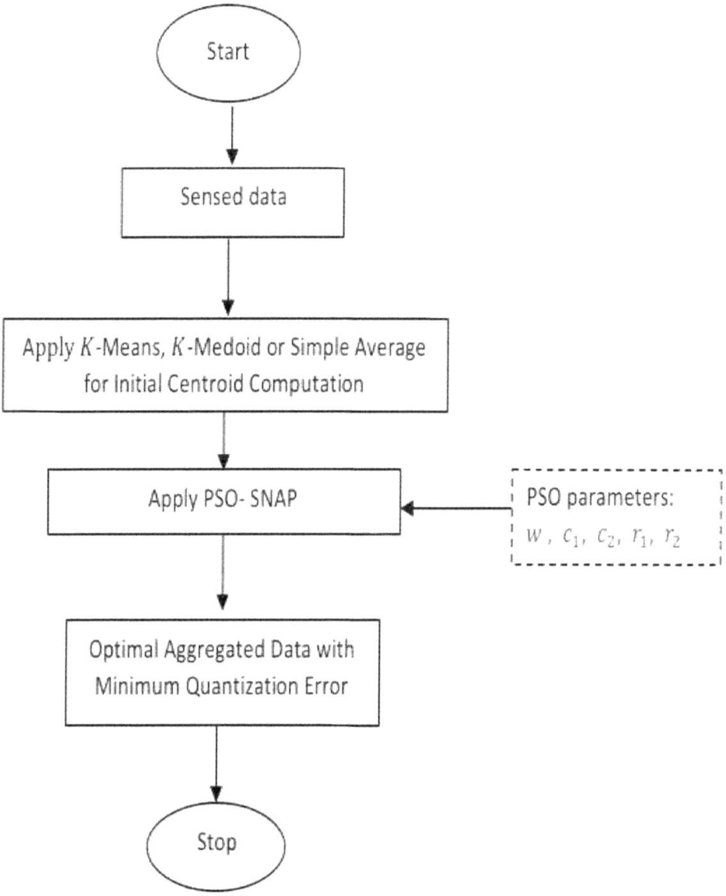

Figure 4.1: Flow chart of the proposed PSO-SNAP

Table 4.1: PSO-SNAP symbolic representations

S.no	Symbol	Description
1	N	Size of data points for aggregation
2	Z_i	The ith data element
3	V_i^t	The data particle velocity at time instance t
4	X_i^t	The data particle position at time instance t
5	$xbest_i^t$	Data particles local best position at time instance t
6	$gbest^t$	Data particles global best position a time instance t
7	w	Inertia weight
8	$c1$	Cognitive constant
9	$c2$	Social constant
10	f^t	The fitness value
11	$r1, r2$	Random numbers
12	M	largest of all the absolute distances of data particle from the particle position
13	α_i	The absolute distance at level i from the particle position
14	n_i	Number of elements in data at an absolute distance α_i for particle position
15	D	The weighted distance of all data elements
16	R	Maximum iterations allowed
17	C	Centroid and the initial position of swarm
18	A	Number of outputs or aggregated values

4.2.1 Algorithm *K*-means

K-means clustering is a partition-based approach for grouping the N input data components in the cluster based on the Euclidean distance from the center point. Each data point is paired with a cluster with a mean. The number of clusters in our suggested PSO-SNAP algorithm is K = 1.

Algorithm 4.1: K-means(N, K)

Input: the size of dataset N, the dataset, number of clusters $K = 1$

Procedure:

1. initialize cluster centroid C randomly
2. repeat:
3. allot all the elements Zi to the cluster with centroid C
4. update the centroid C by calculating the average of all data elements Zi in the cluster
5. until (no change in cluster membership occurs)
6. end-for

Output: Cluster Centroid C

4.2.2 Algorithm *K*-medoid

K-medoid clustering is a partition-based clustering approach based on the sum of dissimilarities between data elements in a cluster group and a point chosen as the cluster's center. As a cluster center, K-medoid identifies data points.

Algorithm 4.2: K-medoid(N, K)

Input: size of dataset N , the dataset, number of clusters K=1

Procedure:

1. initialize cluster centroid C randomly
2. repeat:
3. assign each input data point Zi to the centroid C
4. find medoid and update the cluster centroid C
5. until (no change in cluster membership occurs)
6. end-for

Output: Cluster Centroid C

4.2.3. Particle Swarm Optimization using the weighted fitness function

Particle swarm optimization (PSO) is a metaheuristic search and evolutionary computing method for searching for the best solution to a problem. The collective behavior of a swarm of birds or fish is connected to PSO. A swarm is a large flock of birds. A swarm of possible solutions to an optimization issue is referred to as a swarm in PSO. PSO employs a fitness function as an objective function for determining the best solution. PSO's goal is to determine the swarm's ideal position based on fitness function by iteratively improving data item positions based on better positions found by other data items. The user enters the number of iterations R for which the PSO is repeated. Each data item has its position, which is denoted by X, and velocity, which is denoted by V. The data item position is changed in each iteration using the equations (4.1) and (4.2) below:

$$V_i^{t+1} = wV_i^t + c1r1(xBest_i^t - X_i^t) + c2r2(gBest^t - X_i^t) \quad (4.1)$$

$$X_i^{t+1} = X_i^t + V_i^{t+1} \quad (4.2)$$

Where w, $c1$, $c2$, $r1$, $r2$ are the constants as mentioned in table1.

According to the value of the fitness function stated, the swarm's best global and local position is improved using equations (4.3) and (4.4).

$$xBest_i^{t+1} = \begin{cases} xBest_i^t & if\ f(X_i^{t+1}) \geq f(xBest_i^t) \\ X_i^{t+1} & if\ f(X_i^{t+1}) < f(xBest_i^t) \end{cases} \quad (4.3)$$

$$gBest^{t+1} = xBest_i^{t+1}\ if\ f(xBest_i^{t+1}) < f(gBest^t) \quad (4.4)$$

For the suggested algorithm, the quantization error is used as a fitness function. The quantization error is calculated using the weighted distance between the data elements and the swarm's current best value. The weighted distance of each data from the swarm position is used instead of the Euclidean distance. The weighted distance is derived from the swarm position at three equidistant levels in our experiment, namely α_1, α_2 and α_3. The weighted distance and fitness function are calculated in the following manner.

Step 1: M = maximum $|(Z_i - X_i^t)|\ \forall\ i \in N$

Step 2: $\alpha_1 = M/3$, $\alpha_2 = 2\alpha_1$ and $\alpha_3 = 3\alpha_1$

Step 3: Calculate the values of n_1, n_2, n_3 where n_i = Number of data elements at the absolute difference α_i from the swarm position

Step 4: Calculate weighted distance $D = (\alpha_1 \times n_1 + \alpha_2 \times n_2 + \alpha_3 \times n_3) / N$

Step 5: The quantization error (fitness function) $f^t = \frac{D}{A}$, In our paper value of A is set to 1

4.2.4 Proposed PSO-SNAP Algorithmic Framework

The proposed PSO-SNAP algorithm runs K-means on the input dataset for the first time. The PSO-SNAP method uses the K-means output as its initial centroid. The PSO-SNAP algorithm is run for the number of iterations that the user specifies. The final result is the best value of the swarm position. Apart from K-means, two other methods have been utilized to provide initial input to the PSO-SNAP are K-medoid and a simple mean of the data elements.

The complete PSO-SNAP algorithm is highlighted in Algorithm 4.1.

4.3 EXPERIMENTATION RESULTS AND ANALYSIS

The PSO-SNAP algorithm is implemented in MATLAB using K-means in this part. PSO-SNAP with K-medoid and simple average are two further variations implemented. The number of iterations for which the PSO is repeated is set at R=50 for the sake of experimenting. The constant values are set so that the PSO algorithm achieves higher convergence, with w =0.72, c1 =c2=1.4. The developed PSO-SNAP algorithm is used to analyze real weather data from Dickinson Municipal Airport in Dickinson, North Dakota, in 2009. The sensor node sensed hourly temperature data, which is stored in the dataset. There are 216 entries in the two-dimensional dataset. The new PSO-SNAP method is compared to the conventional PSO-based approach given in the paper [34]. The first 24 data readings from a one-day data set were used for the experiment. The original temperature from the dataset is plotted in Figure 4.2

Algorithm 4.1: PSO-SNAP(N)

Input: Dataset, Size of Dataset (N)

Procedure:

Initialize X_i^t, V_i^t, $xBest_i^t$ to random values and fitness function f^t to infinity

for each data element i = 1 to N

    $X_i^t = C$

end-for

for t = 1 to R

    //calculate fitness value f^t using the steps (a) to (e) given below

    (a) M = maximum $|(Z_i - X_i^t)|$ $\forall$ i $\in$ N

    (b) $\alpha_1 = M/3$, $\alpha_2 = 2\alpha_1$ and $\alpha_3 = 3\alpha_1$

    (c) n_l = Number of data elements at absolute difference α_l from X_i^t, 1<=i<=3

    (d) $D = (\alpha_1 \times n_1 + \alpha_2 \times n_2 + \alpha_3 \times n_3) / N$

    (e) $f^t = \frac{D}{A}$

    for-each data element i = 1 to N

        update local best value $xBest_i^{t+1} = \begin{cases} xBest_i^t & if\ f(X_i^{t+1}) \geq f(xBest_i^t) \\ X_i^{t+1} & if\ f(X_i^{t+1}) < f(xBest_i^t) \end{cases}$

        update global best position $gBest^{t+1} = xBest_i^{t+1}$ $if\ f(xBest_i^{t+1}) < f(gBest^t)$

    end-for

    for-each data element i = 1 to N

        calculate velocity: $V_i^{t+1} = wV_i^t + c_1r_1(xBest_i^t - X_i^t) + c_2r_2(gBest^t - X_i^t)$

        update position: $X_i^{t+1} = X_i^t + V_i^{t+1}$

    end-for

end-for

end

Output: Global best $gBest^t$ position

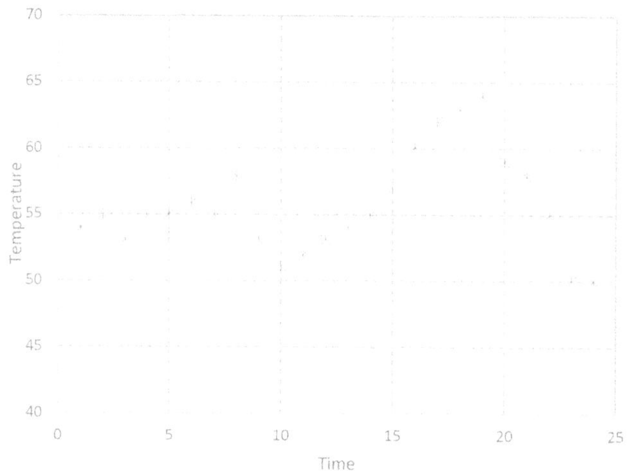

Figure 4.2: Plot of original dataset

The equidistant regions α_1, α_2 *and* α_3 from the centroid are shown in Figure 4.3. It also displays the data items that fall within a specific region.

4.3.1 Proposed PSO-SNAP Outcomes

Table 4.2 shows the results of the performance comparison of the proposed PSO-SNAP with the regular PSO method from paper [34] using three performance parameters: quantization error, aggregated data value, and execution time. The suggested PSO-SNAP algorithm has a quantization error that is 65.4 percent lower than the normal PSO algorithm. Both approaches have comparable aggregated values with minor differences. The proposed PSO-SNAP technique takes 4.18 percent less time to execute than the original PSO algorithm

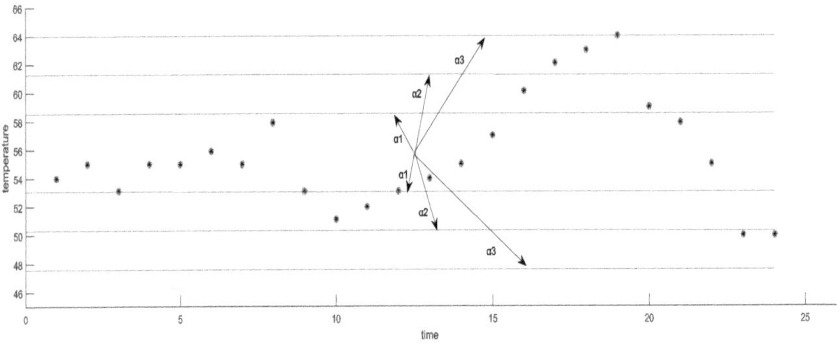

Figure 4.3: Regions $\alpha_1, \alpha_2, \alpha_3$ from the centroid in original dataset

The suggested PSO-SNAP beats the traditional PSO in terms of quantization error and execution time, as shown in the table.

The PSO-SNAP algorithm employing K-means is also tested on input data sets ranging in size from 50 to 200 elements, with a gap of 50 elements. As illustrated in Figure 4.4, the results are compared to the typical PSO algorithm. The graph clearly shows that the presented PSO-SNAP algorithms have less quantization error and faster convergence than the regular PSO method in all circumstances.

Table 4.2: Proposed PSO-SNAP algorithm vs. standard PSO algorithm comparison

Algorithm	Quantization Error	Aggregated Value	Execution Time
PSO algorithm in paper[34]	7.1648	55.6747	6.22
PSO-SNAP with *K*-means	4.3318	55.7924	5.97

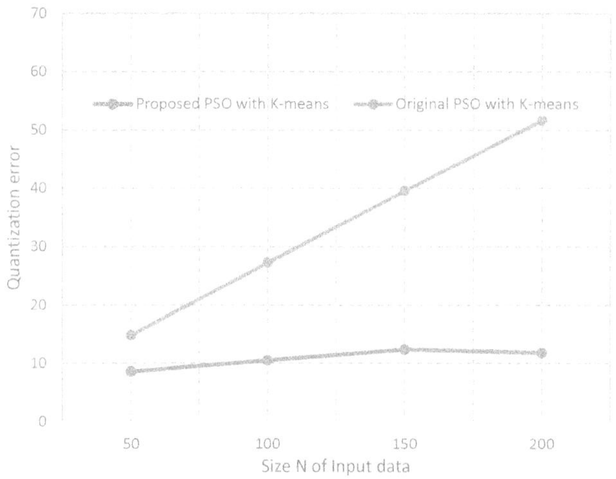

Figure 4.4: Quantization error for PSO-SNAP and regular PSO algorithms with varied input data sizes

4.3.2 Comparative analysis of three versions of PSO-SNAP Algorithm

The K-medoid and simple mean algorithms were used to implement the PSO-SNAP algorithm, and the results were compared. Figure 4.5 shows a comparison of the quantization error of all three proposed techniques. PSO-SNAP with the basic average has a lower quantization error than PSO-SNAP with K-means and PSO-SNAP with K-medoid, implying that the PSO-SNAP technique with a simple average performs better. The final aggregated value obtained by all three variants of the PSO-SNAP algorithm is plotted in Figure 4.6, and the aggregated value generated by PSO-SNAP with K-means is analogous to PSO-SNAP with a simple average. On the one-day data, Figure 4.7 depicts the running time of all three proposed versions of PSO-SNAP. PSO-SNAP with K-means takes less time to execute than the other two versions, PSO-SNAP with simple average and PSO-SNAP with K-medoid. The gross performance of PSO-SNAP with K-means is superior to the other two versions, as shown by the three proposed versions and plots in Figures 4.5, 4.6, and 4.7.

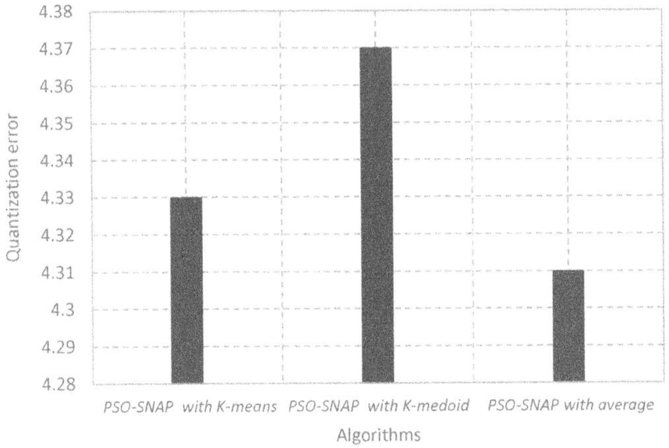

Figure 4.5: Quantization error for proposed PSO-SNAP algorithm all three versions.

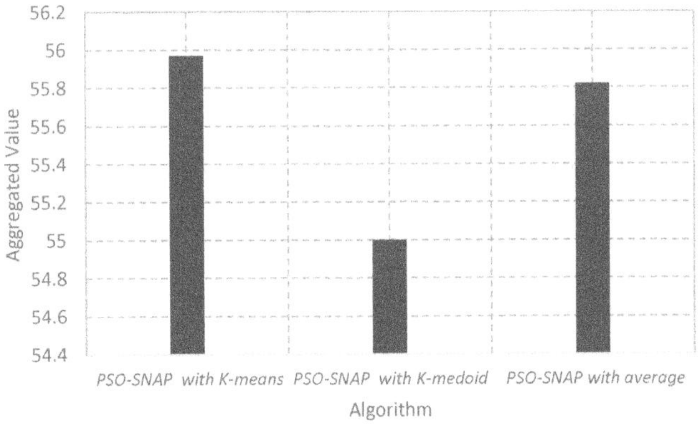

Figure 4.6: Aggregated value for proposed PSO-SNAP algorithm, all three versions

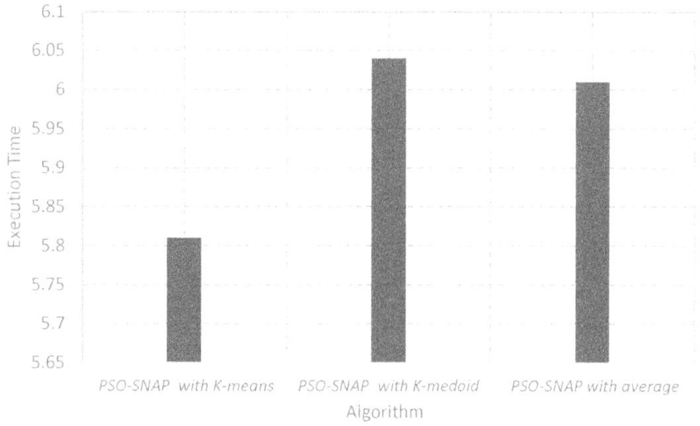

Figure 4.7: Execution time for proposed PSO-SNAP algorithm, all three versions

To examine the pace of growth, all three proposed versions of PSO-SNAP were compared to the rising size of the data. With a gap size of 50, the input sensor dataset ranges from 50 to 200 items. The quantization error is the performance parameter to be compared. The rate of rising of the quantization error for all three variants of PSO-SNAP, namely K-means, K-medoid, and simple average, is plotted in Figure-4.8. In all three implementations, the quantization error is comparable; however, PSO-SNAP with a simple average has a little better value and faster convergence. The execution time of all three variants is plotted against the size of the input data set in Figure 4.9. PSO-SNAP with K-means is moderately faster than the other two versions, PSO-SNAP with K-medoid and PSO-SNAP with a simple average, as shown in the graph. Overall, PSO-SNAP with K-means and PSO-SNAP with simple average perform similarly to PSO-SNAP with K-medoid in terms of convergence and execution time and are better than PSO-SNAP with K-medoid.

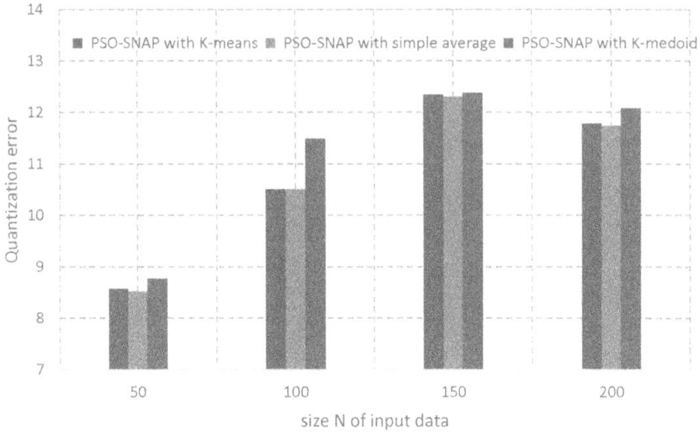

Figure 4.8: Quantization error for proposed PSO-SNAP, all three versions with varied input data sizes

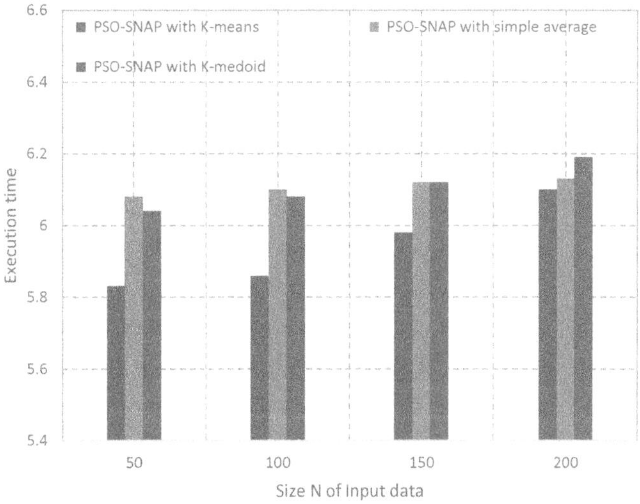

Figure 4.9: Execution time for proposed PSO-SNAP, all three versions with varied input data sizes

4.4 SUMMARY

Reduced energy or battery usage is one of the most crucial design challenges in wireless sensor networks. To reduce the number of packets sent, aggregation of sensed data is required either at the sensor node or the head of the cluster, extending the life of sensor networks. We present a PSO-based weighted data aggregation technique for wireless sensor networks (PSO-SNAP) with input from the K-means, K-medoid, and simple average algorithms in this paper. The proposed PSO-SNAP algorithm features a novel fitness function and seeds the initial input for the swarm using either K-means, K-medoid, or simple average, resulting in better convergence. In comparison to other PSO-based data aggregation algorithms, the suggested PSO-SNAP algorithm has a lower quantization error, a higher value of aggregated data, and a shorter execution time. Quantization error has decreased by 65.4 percent, while execution time has decreased by 4.18 percent. The suggested PSO-SNAP has a faster convergence and execution time, which minimizes WSN power consumption and increases sensor network lifetime. Based on quantization error and execution time, the three proposed versions of PSO-SNAP were compared, and the results were found to be relatively close with just minor differences in values. When comparing the three variants with different input data sizes, it can be determined that PSO-SNAP with K-means and PSO-SNAP with a Simple average have lower quantization error and hence better convergence than PSO-SNAP with K-medoid. However, PSO-SNAP with K-means outperforms the other two versions in terms of execution time. The research can be expanded to include big data aggregation and comparisons with other swarms intelligence-based data aggregation methodologies.

CHAPTER 5
DATA PREDICTION

The third scientific contribution (data prediction) in wireless sensor networks is explained here in this chapter. It explains how the proposed time series-based temperature prediction model works and how it is applied at the sensor node as well as the cluster head. In terms of the amount of data sent from sensor node to cluster head and prediction error, the suggested data prediction model has outperformed benchmark time series-based data, prediction models.

5.1 OVERVIEW

The third scientific contribution (data prediction) in wireless sensor networks is described here. It explains how the proposed time series-based temperature prediction model works and how it is deployed at both the levels, at the sensor node and the head of the cluster. In terms of the number of data transmissions from sensor node to cluster head and prediction error, the suggested data prediction model has outperformed state-of-the-art time series-based data, prediction models.

Weather forecasting, health care, education, stock market analysis, financial banking, customer relationship management, and other applications of data prediction techniques have all had an impact on human life. Weather forecasting and prediction is a fascinating topic with applications in airplane navigation, agriculture, and tourism. To construct prediction models, reveal hidden patterns, and forecast weather conditions, researchers have been drawn to a large amount of weather observation data accessible. Weather prediction is a short-term temperature forecast based on a single parameter (two-dimensional data) and used to forecast a single instance of temperature, such as the temperature of a specific location for the next moment or a few hours later, depending on the application's needs. Weather forecasting, on the other hand, is the prediction of temperature over a lengthy period, such as a few days or even a month. The weather prediction is based on several variables (multidimensional data) such as temperature, air pressure, humidity, and other factors, and it predicts various temperature instances over a period of days or months.

Our research focuses on weather prediction systems that employ sensed data received by sensor network nodes to predict the temperature of the following time instant. A time instance might last anything from one to several hours. Our research intends to reduce repetitive data transmissions to eliminate redundant data transmissions. This saves energy in sensor networks that collect meteorological data before delivering it to the cluster head or sink for processing. The suggested data prediction model is based on the OBV (On-Balance Volume) signal and predicts the temperature of the following time instance in a single parameter time series data. Prediction algorithms can be found in a range of areas, including artificial intelligence, intelligent mining, machine learning, and stock market prediction. The designed On-balance volume indicator-based Data Prediction (ODP) model's symbolic notations, workflow diagram, and methodology are explained in the next section.

5.1.1 Current state-of-art methods

Some state-of-art consumption prediction technique based on linear regression is also used as an efficient technique. In cloud-based data centers, the Linear Regression based prediction technique reduces energy usage. The OBV is being utilized to anticipate changes in stock prices. The OBV indicator as a trading methods for time series data prediction include Linear Regression, Kalman Filter and SVM. Some approaches, such as OBV and ARIMA, are widely utilized in stock prediction. The ARIMA model can be used in a variety of fields, including health care, education, and finance. In thunderstorm forecasting, prediction models such as Support vector machines (SVM) and Rough sets (RS) are utilized, however, they lack high resolution. As a result, RS-SVM, a combination of these two methods, is also, being used. A CPU rule produces great profitability and returns in stock markets.

5.2 PROPOSED OBV BASED DATA PREDICTION MODEL

The developed ODP model, its symbols, and assumptions utilized are described in this section. The highlights of the suggested model are described, as well as the approach in detail.

5.2.1 Proposed ODP Model Assumptions & Notations

The network setup considered here has two levels, with the first level consisting of sensor nodes inside a cluster and the second level consisting of the cluster head. Sensor nodes are in charge of sensing and delivering real-time temperature data to cluster heads, while cluster heads are in charge of receiving data from sensor nodes. At the hardware level, the processor clocks of the sensor node and cluster head are supposed to be synchronized regularly. Table 5.1 shows the symbols that were utilized in the model. For the prediction algorithm, the same version of the developed ODP model is created for both the sensor nodes and cluster head.

Table 5.1: ODP model Symbols and Notations

S.no	Symbol	Description
1	n	Size of the input dataset, index variable i varies from 1 to n
2	e	Parameter predefined and varies from 0.01 to 0.1
3	RT_i	The real temperature sensed by the sensor at timestamp i
4	$RT\_abs\_diff_i$	The absolute difference between two consecutive real temperature recordings
5	FT_i	Final temperature value to be transmitted to the cluster head at timestamp i
6	$FT\_abs\_diff_i$	The absolute difference between two consecutive final temperature recordings at i
7	PT_i	The predicted temperature at timestamp i
8	OBV_i	On-Balance Volume indicator value for i^{th} transmission ($OBV_1 = 0.01$)
9	τ	Wait time at cluster head to receive data from the sensor node

To determine the predicted temperature at the next point in time, the same data prediction approach is used at the sensor node and head of the cluster. The cluster head uses the predicted temperature if the estimated temperature is within the system administrator's temperature tolerance limits, reducing the number of redundant transmission cycles from the sensor node. Otherwise, the cluster head will wait for the temperature measurement from the sensor node.

5.2.2 Model Highlights

The suggested ODP temperature prediction model has the following features:

- Real-time temperature adjustment based on sensed data, which is activated when the expected value exceeds the tolerance limit.
- By decreasing the number of redundant transmissions to the head of the cluster from the sensor node, sensor energy is conserved.
- Improved forecast accuracy while simplifying the model.
- The sensor network's lifetime has been extended.

5.2.3 Proposed ODP Model methodology

The proposed model goes through various processes to calculate the value of the ultimate temperature to be sent to the cluster head. Error tolerance (e) and wait time (τ) are the two predefined parameters that must be set. The maximum variation or difference between the final temperature absolute difference value and the genuine temperature absolute difference value that can be permitted is specified by the error tolerance, which is a preset parameter. It can range from 0.01 to 0.1, depending on the needs of the application. The wait time at the cluster head can be defined as the difference in length between two subsequent sensed temperature values, as well as the overall time required for communication and processing delay by the sensor. If the temperature is sensed every hour by the sensor node, the value can be set to one hour, ignoring communication delays. The following are the steps in the proposed ODP temperature prediction model:

Step 1: Real Timestamped Temperature

The sensor node records the real temperature regularly and is denoted by RT_i, at timestamp i where $i >= 1$. The initial first two values RT_1 and RT_2 are sent to the cluster head.

Step 2: Real Temperature Absolute Difference

This step calculates the absolute difference between two continuous values of real temperature RT_i and RT_{i-1} sensed by the sensor node and denote by $RT\_abs\_diff_i$ where $i > 1$. This is given in the following equation (5.1).

$$RT\_abs\_diff_i = \begin{cases} \left|\frac{RT_i - RT_{i-1}}{RT_{i-1}}\right| & where\ i > 1 \\ undefined & otherwise \end{cases} \tag{5.1}$$

Step 3: Final Temperature Absolute Difference

This step calculates the absolute difference between two continuous values of final temperature values FT_i and FT_{i-1} which is to be sent to the head of the cluster. The final temperature absolute difference is depicted by $FT\_abs\_diff_i$ and the first two initial values are set using real temperature values $FT_1 = RT_1$ and $FT_2 = RT_2$ thereafter using final temperature values FT_i and FT_{i-1} as shown in equation (5.2).

$$FT\_abs\_diff_i = \begin{cases} \left|\frac{FT_i - FT_{i-1}}{FT_{i-1}}\right| where\ i > 1 \\ undefined\ otherwise \end{cases} \tag{5.2}$$

Step 4: On Balance Volume Indicator

The on-balance volume indicator's value, abbreviated as OBV_i. The value of OBV_1 is initially set to 0.01. To obtain the next value of OBV_i, compare the two continuous final temperature values; if the next final temperature value is greater than the previous value, add the final temperature absolute difference to the previous OBV_{i-1} value. Remove the absolute value of the final temperature difference value from the previous OBV_{i-1} value if the next final temperature value is lower than the previous one; otherwise, the OBV value does not change, as shown in equation (5.3).

$$OBV_i = \begin{cases} OBV_{i-1} & if\ (FT_i == FT_{i-1}) \\ OBV_{i-1} + FT\_abs\_diff_i & if(FT_i > FT_{i-1}) \\ OBV_{i-1} - FT_{abs_{diff}\,i} & if(FT_i < FT_{i-1}) \end{cases} \quad (5.3)$$

Step 5: Predicted Temperature

The predicted temperature is denoted as PT_i is calculated in this step. The next timestamped value of predicted temperature PT_i is obtained by adding the OBV_i value to the previous final temperature as mentioned in the following equation (5.4).

$$PT_i = \begin{cases} undefined & where\ i = 1 \\ FT_{i-1} + OBV_i & where\ i > 1 \end{cases} \quad (5.4)$$

Step 6: Final Temperature

In this step, designated by FT_i finds the final temperature measurements to be conveyed to the cluster head. The first two values, FT_1 and T_2 , correspond to RT_1 and RT_2 respectively. The final temperature value is either the actual temperature or the prior value of the projected temperature. By comparing the highest of $RT\_abs\_diff_i$ and $FT\_abs\_diff_i$ with the error tolerance, the next value of final temperature FT_i is computed. The next timestamped value of the final temperature equals the real temperature if the maximum surpasses the error tolerance; alternatively, it equals the previous value of the projected temperature.

The cluster head uses the final temperature calculated in equation (5.5).

$$FT_i = \begin{cases} RT_i & where\ i \leq 2 \\ RT_i\ \ if\ (\max(FT\_abs\_diff_{i-1}, RT\_abs\_diff_{i-1}) > e\ and\ i > 2 \\ PT_{i-1}\ \ if\ (\max(FT\_abs\_diff_{i-1}, RT\_abs\_diff_{i-1}) < e\ \ and\ i > 2 \end{cases} \quad (5.5)$$

The final temperature value FT_i is used to assess whether the sensor node's temperature value must be conveyed to the head of the cluster or whether the head of the cluster can use the model's previous projected temperature value. The cluster head will receive the real temperature measurement from the sensor node if $FT_i = RT_i$, else, no transmission will occur, leading to energy reduction. The cluster head also calculates the expected temperature value at periodic intervals and needs to wait to receive data from the sensor node for a set period; if the actual temperature value is not received from the sensor node, the next timestamped temperature is the temperature predicted by the model.

Figure 5.1 depicts the flow chart of the developed ODP model at the sensor. As discussed in the preceding section, the model operates in six steps. When these processes are completed in the correct order, the final temperature may be predicted, reducing the requirement for several data transmissions to the cluster head during a single data collection cycle. The proposed model's flow diagram at the cluster head is shown in Figure 5.2. To complete the prediction process, the model implemented at the cluster head only requires three steps numbered 3 to 5.

5.3 EXPERIMENTATION RESULTS AND ANALYSIS

The experimental findings achieved by using the suggested ODP model for temperature prediction are discussed in this section. Our suggested approach is also compared against benchmark models like linear regression and the ARIMA model for performance.

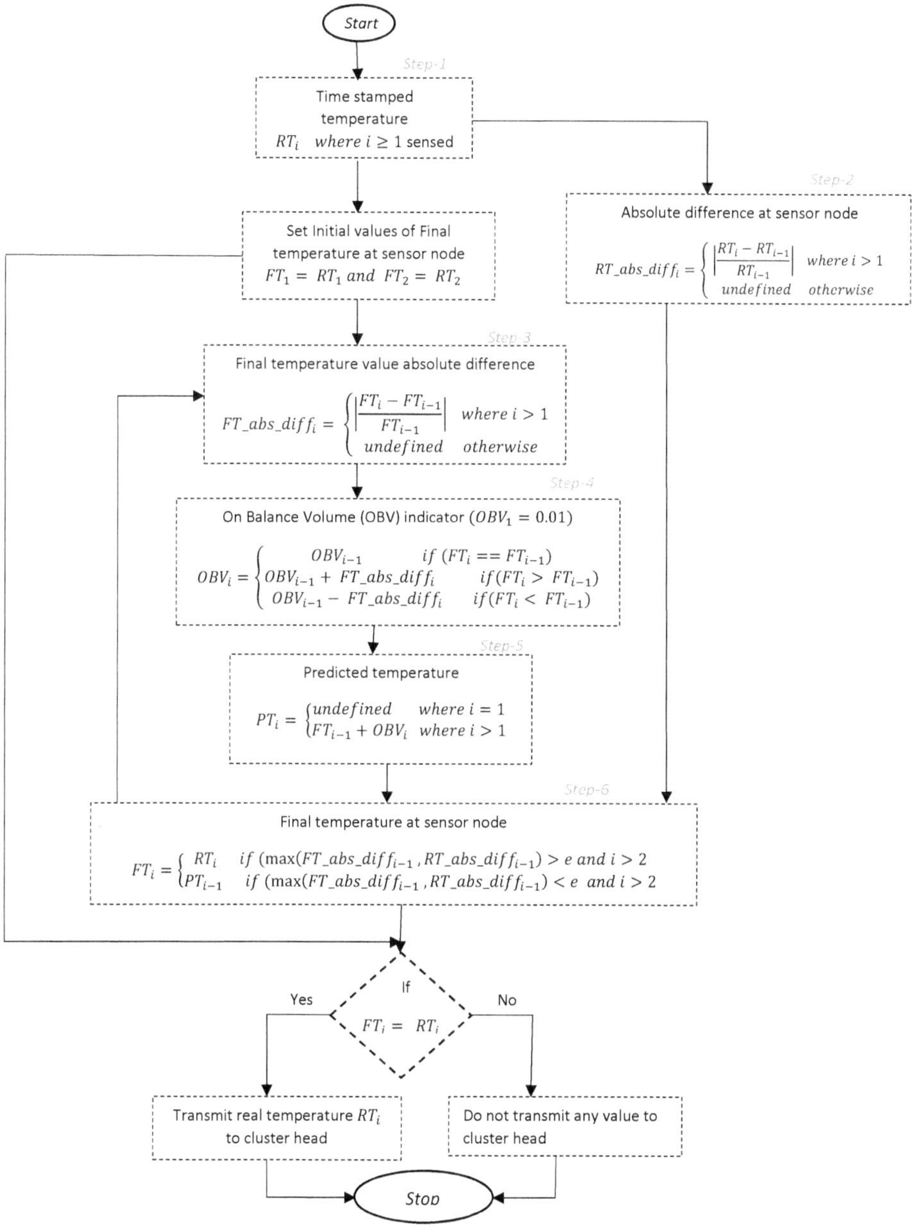

Figure -5.1: Proposed ODP prediction model at sensor node

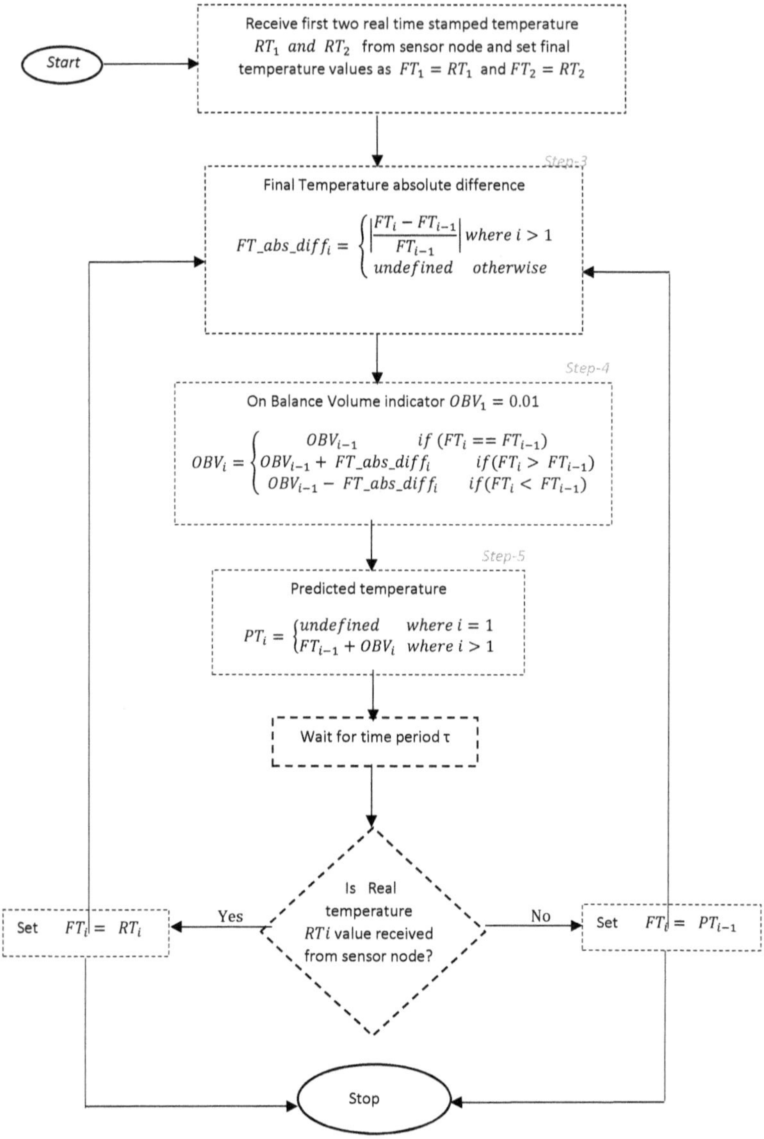

Figure-5.2: Proposed ODP prediction model at cluster head

5.3.1 Proposed ODP Model Outcomes

The suggested model is used to analyze real temperature data from Dickinson Municipal Airport in Dickinson, North Dakota, and the United States for the year 2009. Hourly temperature data obtained by a sensor node during 9 days is included in the weather dataset. There are 216 entries in the two-dimensional dataset. As a result, the wait time value is set to one hour while transmission delay is ignored. A plot of real temperature RTi and anticipated temperature PTi with a tolerance value of 0.03 is shown in Figure 5.3. The anticipated temperature values, as can be seen, are very similar to the actual temperature measured by the sensor.

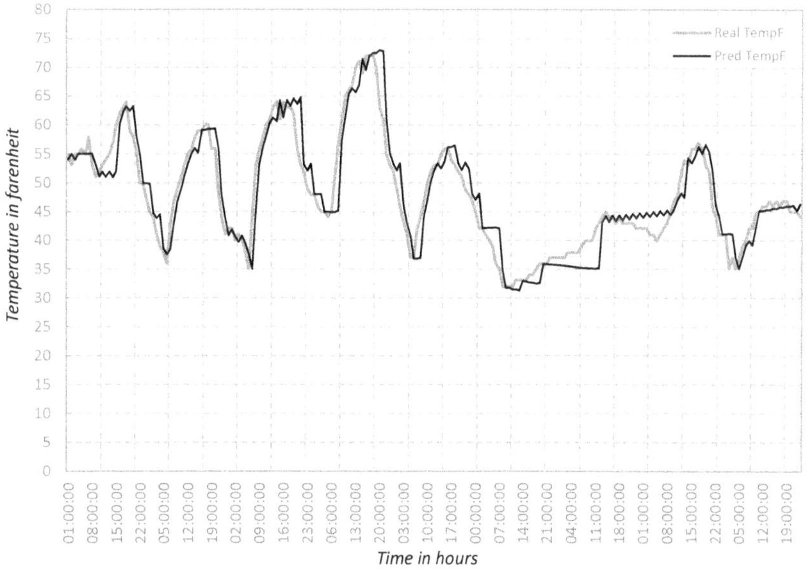

Figure 5.3: Comparative analysis of real & predicted temperature

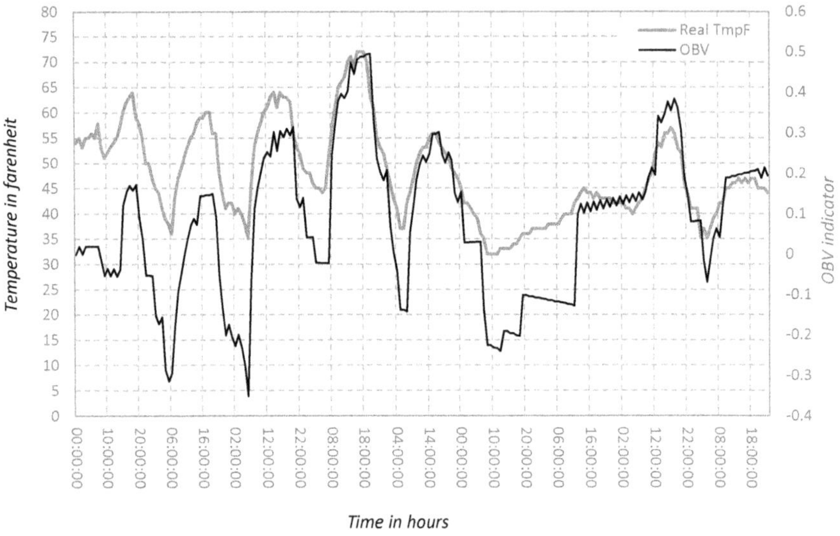

Figure 5.4: Real-time temperature & OBV measurements comparison

A plot of OBV values versus actual temperature data is shown in Figure 5.4. The temperature values predicted by OBV are quite similar to the actual temperatures. The OBV indicator rises as the temperature rises and reduces as the temperature declines, as shown in the graph. The OBV value becomes negative when the temperature lowers abruptly, and vice versa. A tolerance level of 0.03 is used in the plot.

The absolute difference between actual and finalized temperature measurements is depicted in Figure 5.5. The hourly change in temperature measurements is depicted in the graph that results. The final temperature is shown to be quite near to the real temperature, with only slight changes in values. The number of times the prediction model accurately forecasts the final temperature without requiring new temperature information to be delivered to the head of the cluster is known as the model's accuracy. The correctness of the model is determined by the tolerance percentage. As the tolerance spans from 0.1 to 0.01 the forecast accuracy improves. This, on the other hand, results in greater disparities between actual and anticipated temperature values, increasing the prediction error. As a result, there is a compromise between tolerance and temperature accuracy predictions.

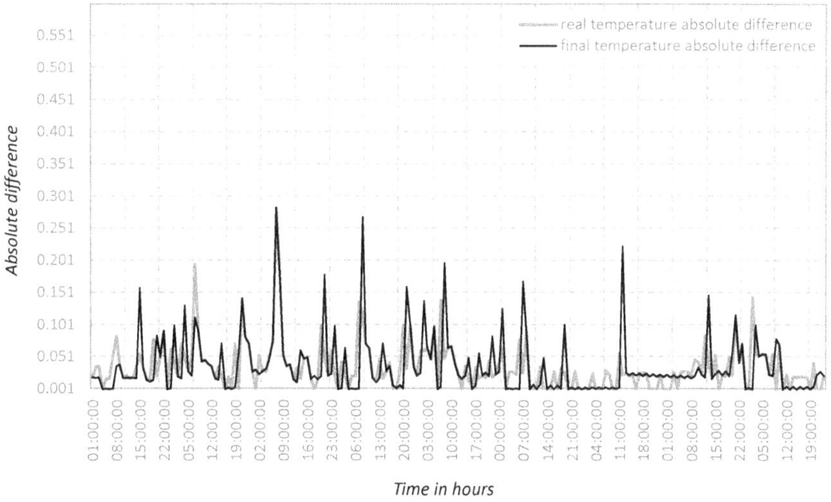

Figure 5.5: Absolute difference of real & final temperature

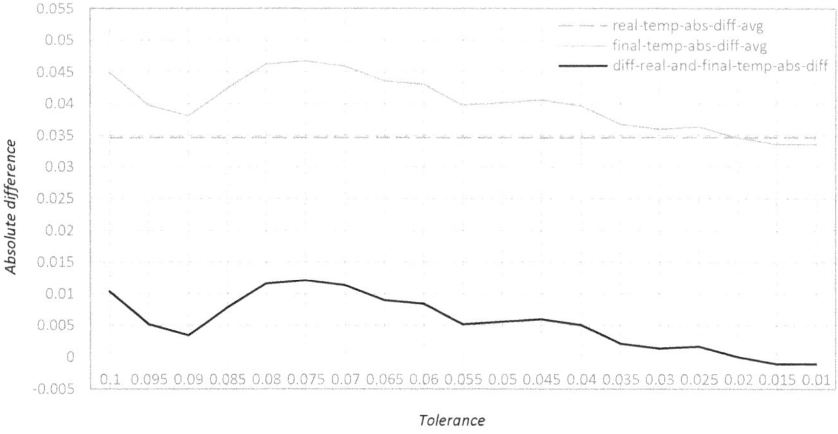

Figure 5.6: Error tolerance versus average values of absolute differences

The average values of the real temperature absolute difference and the final temperature absolute difference are plotted in Figure 5.6 as the tolerance percentage is changed from 0.01 to 0.1. The difference between the two averages is also depicted on the plot at various tolerance percentages. At a tolerance of 0.03, the average values are identical, and the difference is highest at 0.1. Figure 5.7 shows how the average of the absolute difference in final temperature evolves with tolerance and the initial value of OBV is a multi-dimensional representation. The OBV has tolerance and an initial value of 0.01 to 0.1. The graph demonstrates that for different values of OBV and tolerance, the average absolute difference in final temperature is lowest when OBV is 0.01 and tolerance is 0.03. With a larger percentage of accurate temperature prediction and a higher similarity between real and expected temperatures, the ideal values of the specified parameter for tolerance are 0.03 and the initial value of the OBV indicator is 0.01. This explains why the initial tolerance value of 0.03 was chosen.

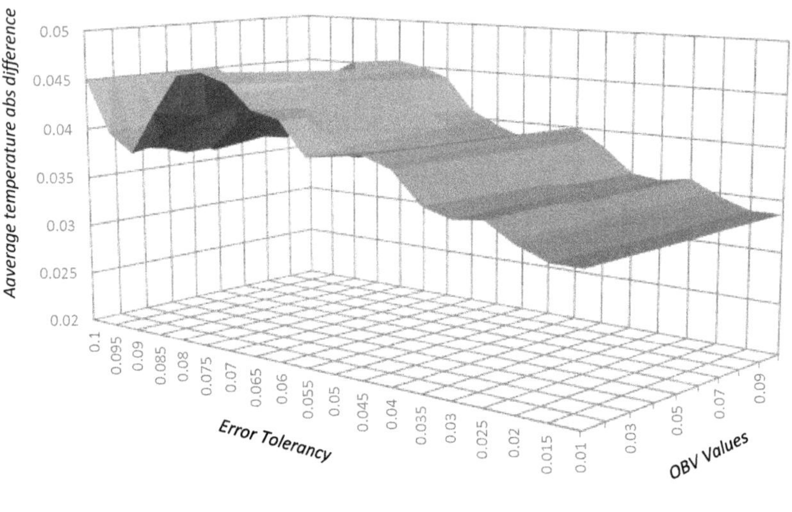

Figure 5.7: Effect of variation in OBV and tolerance on final temperature absolute difference

5.3.2 Comparative Analysis

Linear Regression and Auto-regressive Integrated Moving Average (ARIMA) benchmark models are used to evaluate the proposed ODP model.

(a) **Linear Regression (LR):** It is the most frequent statistical tool for modeling the relationship among variables. It is determined using the equation $y = a + bx$, where a is the y-intercept, which is the mean value of y when all x variables are equal to zero and is measured using the equation, $a = \bar{y} - b\bar{x}$. The slope of a regression line, which shows the rate of change for y as x changes, is determined using the equation, $b = \frac{\sum(x-\bar{x})(y-\bar{y})}{\sum(x-\bar{x})^2}$ in this case. The starting values of a and b are derived using the known values of x and y used for prediction.

(b) **ARIMA:** The ARIMA model is a prominent and commonly used statistical tool for time series forecasting and analysis. Autoregressive Integrated Moving Average (ARIMA) is an acronym for Autoregressive Integrated Moving Average. It is a type of model that can capture a wide range of conventional temporal structures in time series data. You may forecast and analyze a time series using past values by employing an ARIMA model, such as projecting future prices based on historical revenues. These types of univariate models are used to better comprehend a single time-dependent variable in the data, such as temperature across time. These models assume that the data is stationary. The parameters p,d and q are a typical notation for characterizing ARIMA. The parameters are rapidly replaced with an integer number to indicate which ARIMA model is being utilized. The ARIMA model parameters are further explained as follows:

AR (p) Autoregression – It is a regression model that takes advantage of the dependent relationship between a current observation and prior data. The usage of past values in the regression equation for the time series is referred to as an autoregressive (AR (p)) component. It is also known as the lag order, and it refers to the number of lag observations incorporated in the model.

I (d) Integration – It makes the time series stationary by differencing observations (subtracting an observation from the previous time step). Differencing is the process of subtracting a series' current values from its prior values d times. The degree of difference refers to the number of times the raw observations are distinguished.

MA (q) Moving Average – It takes advantage of the relationship between an observation and the residual error from a moving average model applied to lagged data. A moving average component represents the model's error as a sum of prior error terms. The number of words to be included in the model is represented by the order q.

The reason for selecting ARIMA (1,1,0) model is that the proposed ODP model for temperature prediction in a sensor network uses one past observation to predict the next value hence in the ARIMA model the autoregression coefficient (p) has been taken as 1. The degree of differencing in the ODP model is one hence in ARIMA the value of the Integration coefficient is taken as one. The moving average coefficient (q) is taken as 0 since there is no dependency between the observation and residual error in the proposed model.

The two performance parameters used for comparative analysis are as follows:

(i) Error in prediction: The difference between the predicted temperatures and actual temperature is defined as prediction error. Figure 5.8 depicts the error plots for temperature for all three models (a-c). Figure 5.8(a) depicts the proposed ODP model's prediction error plot, which reveals that it has the least error deviation from zero line, whereas Figure 5.8(b) depicts the ARIMA model's error plot, which exhibits a larger discrepancy from the zero-line. Figure 5.8(c) depicts the LR model error plot with the greatest divergence from the zero-line. Figure 5.8(d) depicts the combined error plot of all three models, demonstrating that the new ODP model is justified by the superior performance since LR is more divergent than ARIMA. Whereas LR has highest error in prediction and least performance among all the three models. The proposed ODP model gives the best performance when the error tolerance is taken as 0.03. At this point difference between the temperature predicted by the ODP model and the actual temperature sensed by the sensor node is having least difference in values, hence the proposed model make the correct prediction at the cluster head also, so need of temperature data transmission from sensor node to cluster head. The proposed model makes the real time adjustment with the real data stream from time to time, to reduce the error in prediction .

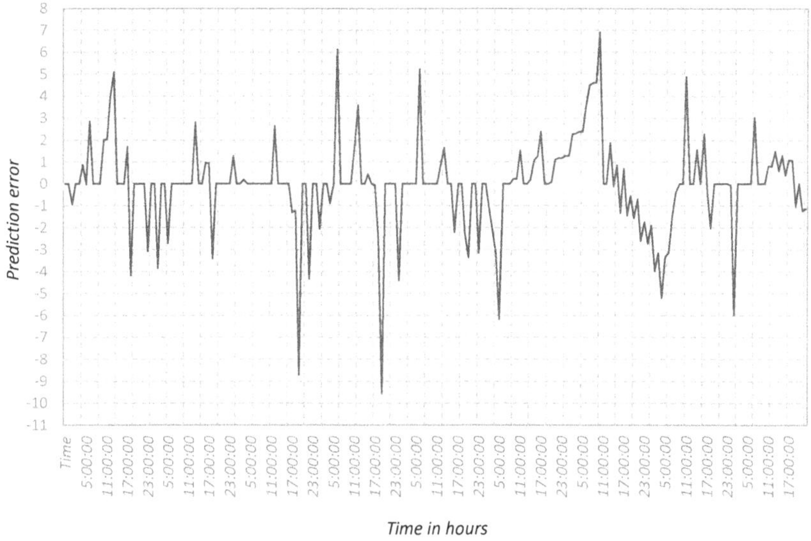

Figure 5.8(a): Prediction error in proposed ODP model

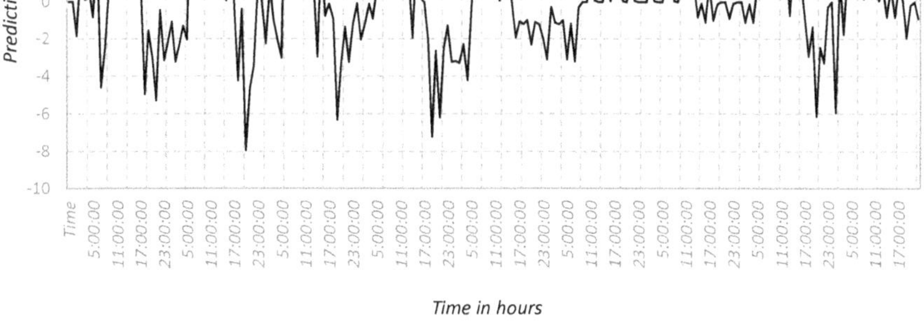

Figure 5.8(b): Prediction error in ARIMA model

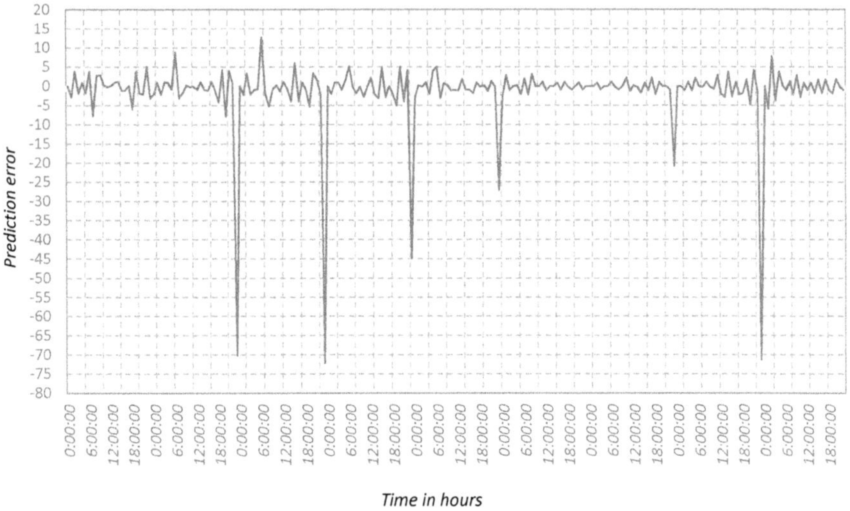

Figure 5.8(c): Prediction error in LR model

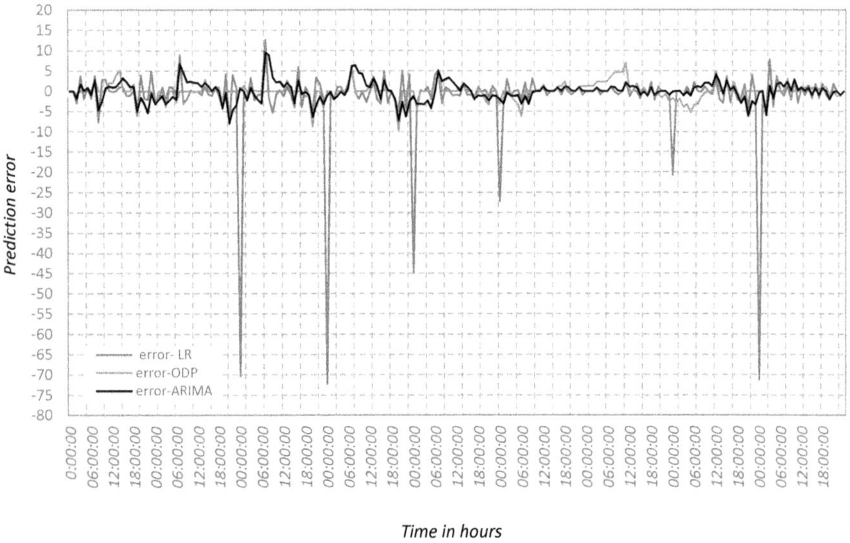

Figure 5.8(d): Combined prediction error in proposed ODP, LR, & ARIMA model

(ii) Number of Transmissions: Figure 5.9 depicts the number of transmissions saved for the proposed ODP model based on different tolerance error values. It can be seen that with 0.03 error tolerance, our proposed ODP model saves 50% of transmissions. As the error tolerance level is dropped from 0.1 to 0.01, the number of transmissions from the sensor node increases, resulting in increased energy usage. Increasing the error tolerance level from 0.01 to 0.1 reduces the number of transmissions from the sensor node but at the cost of higher inaccuracy. Using the ARIMA model, Figure 5.10 displays the number of transmissions for various amounts of error tolerance. The result shows that the model survived until 0.05, after which it had to perform 100 percent transmissions, resulting in 0 percent energy savings, and the prediction accuracy falls short of the real value, necessitating the transmission of information. When compared to our proposed research, this results in higher energy consumption. Figure 5.11 depicts the number of transmissions with varying error tolerances for the LR model. Despite the fact that the LR model survives the decrease in error tolerance, it fails to preserve sensor energy, which is depleted due to the higher number of transmissions than our ODP method. Only 9.25 percent of transmissions could be saved with an error tolerance of 0.03. Furthermore, our research initiative contributes to a 50% reduction in the total transmission of data from the node to the head of the cluster, resulting in significant power savings.

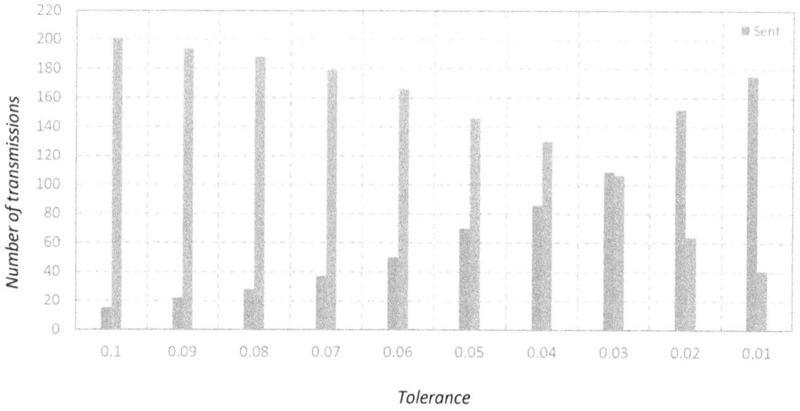

Figure 5.9: Number of transmissions for proposed ODP model with varied error tolerance

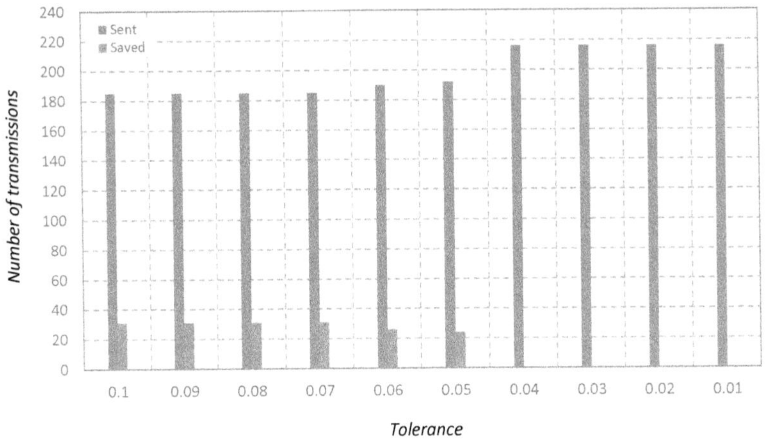

Figure 5.10: Number of transmissions for ARIMA model with varied error tolerance

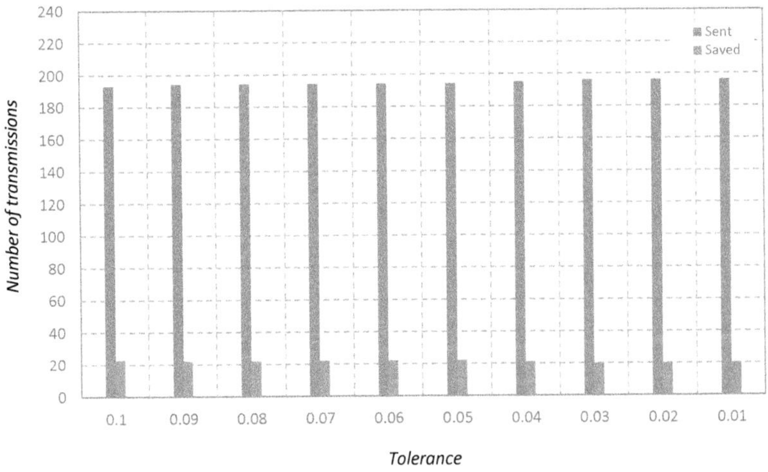

Figure 5.11: Number of transmissions for LR model with varied error tolerance

5.4 SUMMARY

Energy is a vital resource to manage and use because these sensor nodes are power-constrained devices. To maximize network longevity without jeopardizing sensor operation, the energy must be used efficiently. The use of data prediction to reduce the transmission of sensor information from the cluster members (sensors) to the cluster head or sink is a useful technique. For temperature prediction in sensor networks, we offer a new On-balance-volume indicator-based Data Prediction (ODP) model. Our prediction model employs the OBV indicator, which is frequently utilized in stock market forecasting. At both the sensor node and the cluster head, the proposed model has been implemented. The findings show that by carefully selecting error tolerances, the model may produce reliable results with a 50% accuracy while sacrificing little between real and forecast temperature values. Additionally, the new ODP model is compared to two benchmark models, the ARIMA and Linear Regression models, in terms of assessment parameters. As the error tolerance range changes, these parameters essentially involve the prediction error and the number of transmissions stored. The experimental results suggest that our developed ODP model outperforms the ARIMA and Linear Regression models in terms of performance evaluation parameters. In the event of a substantial prediction error, our suggested approach can accomplish data synchronization by replacing obsolete projected data with real-time sensory data.

CHAPTER 6

DATA SECURITY

This chapter presents the fourth research contribution (security of data) in wireless sensor networks. This chapter explains the methodology of the proposed enhanced version of the AES encryption algorithm. The suggested enhanced AES encryption algorithm has been proven effective against standard AES encryption algorithms as well as other data encryption algorithms in terms of execution time and energy consumption.

6.1 OVERVIEW

WSNs are infrastructural-free networks that are typically deployed in hazardous, unsupervised, and unmanaged situations. Anyone or attackers can easily break into wireless networks and listen in on vital and sensitive communications via a radio interface since they are open networks. As a result, providing security mechanisms in WSN to protect data from malicious attacks is critical. Because of its limited resources, WSN poses a significant security challenge. WSNs have a variety of security needs, including data secrecy, data validity, the integrity of data, non-repudiation, availability of data, and data freshness. The processing power, battery power, and memory of WSNs are limited. As a result, energy-efficient security methods must be integrated into each component to produce a complete security system. Low computing power, limited memory, and limited battery power are all requirements for WSNs, which makes information security in WSNs difficult. Cryptography is a useful method for securing data in sensor networks. It is critical to choose an appropriate cryptographic algorithm that meets the constraints of WSNs. Cryptographic algorithms employed in WSNs should be evaluated based on the size of the code, the size of the data, the processing time, and the power consumption, as well as the limits of sensor nodes. Due to the computational and memory limitations of sensor nodes, typical cryptography algorithms cannot be easily ported to WSNs. As a result, to meet the aforementioned security criteria, existing approaches must be adapted or new techniques must be invented. We can divide them into two categories based on known cryptography algorithms: public key (asymmetric) encryption methods and private key (symmetric) encryption methods are two types of cryptographic methods.

The use of a public key or asymmetric algorithm approaches like the RSA and Diffie-Hellman algorithms in WSNs is undesired due to the intricacy of the code, the size of the data, the processing time, and the power consumption. The majority of the encryption approaches in WSN apply only symmetric or private key cryptography because they can be easily implemented on less hardware and has low power consumption.

Our study begins with a review of ground-breaking progress in symmetric cryptographic approaches in sensor networks. For providing security to information transmitted in WSN, The symmetric cryptographic methods, including DES (Data Encryption Standard), AES (Advanced Encryption Standard), RC5 (Rivest Cipher), and Blowfish, exist for ensuring security to information conveyed. We report the findings of a proposed modification to the AES encryption method.

6.1.1 Current state-of-art methods

There are certain benchmark methods for implementing data security in sensor networks. For instance, some methods employ symmetric cryptographic algorithms such as Triple DES (Data Encryption Standard), AES (Advanced Encryption Blowfish is lengthy, subkeys must be computed ahead of time. When various factors such as data Standard), RC5 (Rivest Cipher), and Blowfish. Blowfish is faster than AES and 3DES, according to these papers, however, it requires a lot of memory, thus it cannot be used in smart cards. In terms of energy usage and throughput, the blowfish outperforms triple-DES and AES. Because the key generation procedure for type, data density, data size, and key size are considered, AES outperforms 3DES and blowfish. AES is by far the most popular technique for data encryption in sensor networks. AES has been improved and enhanced by using the concept of key dependent S-box, parallel implementaiton of AES on multiprocessor. The improved hardware version of AES using reversible logic gates is also been used in WSN. AES is a fast encryption technique that may be utilized across multiple platforms, including embedded devices. AES offers easy and quick installation in hardware and software.

6.2 PROPOSED ENHANCED AES METHODOLOGY

The Advanced Encryption Standard (AES) is the widely used standard encryption method in wireless sensor networks. The AES technique is well-known for its speed, software and hardware compatibility, and ease of implementation. We assumed that some sensor nodes were heterogeneous, meaning that they had greater processing and communication power than the rest of the network. Rather than being a Feistel cipher, AES is an iterative cryptographic algorithm, which makes use of a substitution–permutation network for encryption. It is made up of a series of interconnected processes, some of which require replacing defined outputs for specified inputs (substitutions) and others, which involve shifting bits around (permutations). AES computes all of its calculations in bytes, not in bits. As a result, AES treats 128 bits of plaintext as 16 bytes. These 16 bytes are divided into four columns and four rows for matrix processing. Unlike DES, AES allows users to adjust the number of rounds, which is determined by the key length. Three different block ciphers are used by AES:

128 bit AES, which uses a 128-bit key size to encrypt and decrypt a block of message.

192 bit AES, which uses a 192-bit key size to encrypt and decrypt a block of communications.

256 bit AES, which uses a 256-bit key size, to encrypt and decrypts a block of message.

Using encryption key sizes of 128 bit, 192 bit, and 256 bits, each algorithm encrypts and decrypts data in 128-bit blocks. Symmetric encryption, often known as secret key cryptographic algorithms, uses the same key to encrypt and decrypt data. The secret key must be known by both the sender and the receiver. It takes ten rounds to encrypt the data with a 128-bit key, twelve rounds to encrypt the data with a 192-bit key, and fourteen rounds to encrypt the data with a 256-bit key. To produce the final ciphertext output, a round consists of many processing steps that include substitution, transposition, and mixing of the columns of input plaintext. Figure 6.1 depicts the AES encryption algorithm's flow diagram. The *Nr* represents the number of rounds. Each round of AES has four steps

- **Substitute bytes**: This is when the substitute is put into action. Each byte is replaced by another byte in this stage. (A lookup table, commonly known as the S-box, is used.) This substitution is done in such a way that a byte is never substituted by itself, nor by another byte that complements the present byte. As before, the result of this step is a 16 byte (4 x 4) matrix.

- **Shift rows**: This step is exactly what it says on the tin. A certain number of times each row is shifted. The initial row is not shifted in any way. The second row is relocated to the left once more. The third row has been relocated to the left twice. The fourth row has been relocated to the left twice. All this is done with a left circular shift.
- **Mix Columns:** This is essentially a matrix multiplication step. Each column is multiplied by a specified matrix, resulting in a change in the position of each byte in the column. Every column having four bytes is modified using a specific mathematical function. This function takes four bytes from one column as input and replaces them with four new bytes. In the output, a new matrix is produced with 16 more bytes. It is worth mentioning that in the final round, this stage is bypassed.
- **Add Round key:** The round key's 128 bits are XORed with the matrix's 16 bytes, which are now considered 128 bits. If this is the final round, the cipher text is output. Otherwise, the 128 bits are translated into 16 bytes, and the procedure is repeated.

Decrypting an AES cipher text in reverse is similar to the reverse process of encryption. Each cycle is made up of four processes mentioned above, which are carried out in the opposite sequence. The add round key is the first step, then Mix Columns, third step is shift rows and the last step is substitution bytes. The number of rounds for decryption is same as number of rounds applied in encryption of data. The same set of keys are used in decryption. A separate key expansion algorithm is used for generating keys for all rounds of AES algorithm staring with the original AES key. The AES encryption is used in many applications such as encrypted browsing, processor security, wireless security, and general file encryption for transferring files, chat messages, legal documents and family pictures. AES is the most widely used encryption technique even today.

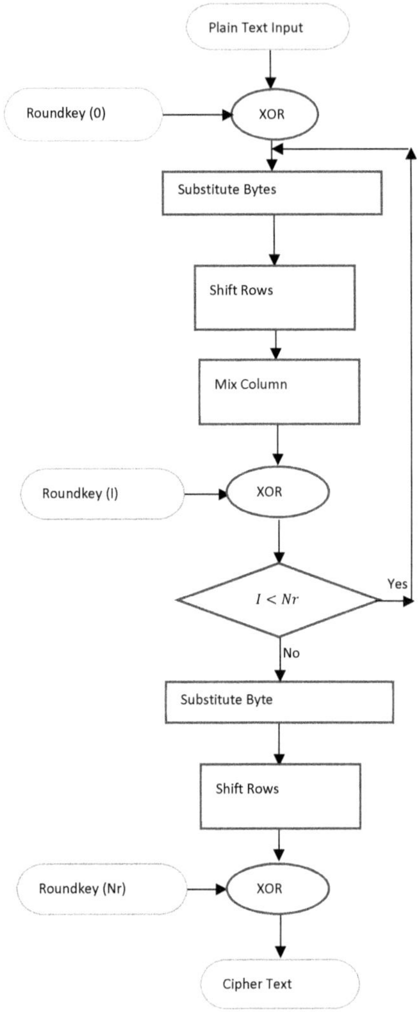

Figure 6.1: The AES encryption algorithm's program flow diagram

6.2.1. Enhanced AES Overview

The substitution box (S-Box) is a look-up table used by the bytes replacing step of the encryption method to substitute the 16 bytes of the input plaintext block. This Substitution-box look-up table is time taking process since AES substitutes one byte at a time. There hasn't been much progress in this area in terms of reducing the time necessary for byte-by-byte substitution using an S-box table and improving the algorithm's efficiency. The initial 128 bytes of the AES 256-byte S-box are divided into two portions, one holding the first 128 bytes and the other containing the remaining 128 bytes, according to our study plan. If two bytes occur in different S-boxes, they can be substituted at the same time when using S-Box substitution; otherwise, the look-up will be serial. It lengthens the algorithm's execution time and so improves its efficiency. This technique will also conserve energy because it will require fewer CPU cycles for encryption than the standard technique. The suggested approach will be advantageous in hierarchical multi-core heterogeneous wireless sensor networks since these networks use clustering and the cluster head is more efficient than a standard node.

The concept of multithreading is used to support parallel programming at the input block level. For parallel S-Box substitution, the proposed work employs two threads. Figures 6.2 and 6.3 depict the S-boxes for our proposed scheme, respectively.

	0	1	2	3	4	5	6	7	8	9	A	B	C	D	E	F
0	6	7	7	7	F	6	6	C	3	0	6	2	F	D	A	7
	3	C	7	B	2	B	F	5	0	1	7	B	E	7	B	6
1	C	8	C	7	F	5	4	F	A	D	A	A	9	A	7	C
	A	2	9	D	A	9	7	0	D	4	2	F	C	4	2	0
2	B	F	9	2	3	3	F	C	3	A	E	F	7	D	3	1
	7	D	3	6	6	F	7	C	4	5	5	1	1	8	1	5
3	0	C	2	C	1	9	0	9	0	1	8	E	E	2	B	7
	4	7	3	3	8	6	5	A	7	2	0	2	B	7	2	5
4	0	8	2	1	1	6	5	A	5	3	D	B	2	E	2	8
	9	3	C	A	B	E	A	0	2	B	6	3	9	3	F	4
5	5	D	0	E	2	F	B	5	6	C	B	3	4	4	5	C
	3	1	0	D	0	C	1	B	A	B	E	9	A	C	8	F
6	D	E	A	F	4	4	3	8	4	F	0	7	5	3	9	A
	0	F	A	B	3	D	3	5	5	9	2	F	0	C	F	8
7	5	A	4	8	9	9	3	F	B	B	D	2	1	F	F	D
	1	3	0	F	2	D	8	5	C	6	A	1	0	F	3	2

Figure 6.2: S-box-1 after splitting approach

	0	1	2	3	4	5	6	7	8	9	A	B	C	D	E	F
8	C D	0 C	1 3	E C	5 F	9 7	4 4	1 7	C 4	A 7	7 E	3 D	6 4	5 D	1 9	7 3
9	6 0	8 1	4 F	D C	2 2	2 A	9 0	8 8	4 6	E E	B 8	1 4	D E	5 E	0 B	D B
A	E 0	3 2	3 A	0 A	4 9	0 6	2 4	5 C	C 2	D 3	A C	6 2	9 1	9 5	E 4	7 9
B	E 7	C 8	3 7	6 D	8 D	D 5	4 E	A 9	6 C	5 6	F 4	E A	6 5	7 A	A E	0 8
C	B A	7 8	2 5	2 E	1 C	A 6	B 4	C 6	E 8	D D	7 4	1 F	4 B	B D	8 B	8 A
D	7 0	3 E	B 5	6 6	4 8	0 3	F 6	0 E	6 1	3 5	5 7	B 9	8 6	C 1	1 D	9 E
E	E 1	F 8	9 8	1 1	6 9	D 9	8 E	9 4	9 B	1 E	8 7	E 9	C E	5 5	2 8	D F
F	8 C	A 1	8 9	0 D	B F	E 6	4 2	6 8	4 1	9 9	2 D	0 F	B 0	5 4	B B	1 6

Figure 6.3: S-box-2 after splitting approach

6.2.2 Working model of the Enhanced-AES

Two bytes of the input state matrix are verified at a time during S-box replacement; if they are in different S-boxes, they are replaced concurrently at the same time; if not, the procedure is serial. An example of an input state matrix that holds bytes in hexadecimal format is shown in Figure 4. They can be substituted in parallel because byte 37 is in S-box-1 and byte 90 is in S-box-2. If a one-time unit is required for each byte. The 16 bytes will take 16 time units to process. The suggested approach, on the other hand, allows the full matrix to be substituted in parallel, decreasing the replacement execution time for the input matrix illustrated in Figure 4 from 16 to 10 entries. This procedure will be repeated for each iteration of the algorithm. Furthermore, the parallel operation consumes fewer CPU cycles than the original serial process, resulting in decreased power usage.

With the help of an example in figure 6.4, the technique is outlined below. The presented work model for one round of substitution is shown in Figure 6.5. This section summarizes the experimental findings that validate the increased effectiveness of the suggested Enhanced-AES (EAES) approach for conserving sensor energy and thereby extending the sensor network's useful lifetime.

37	90	72	AB
BC	32	57	DA
41	FE	F0	29
AC	84	CD	A8

Figure 6.4: An example of the input state matrix

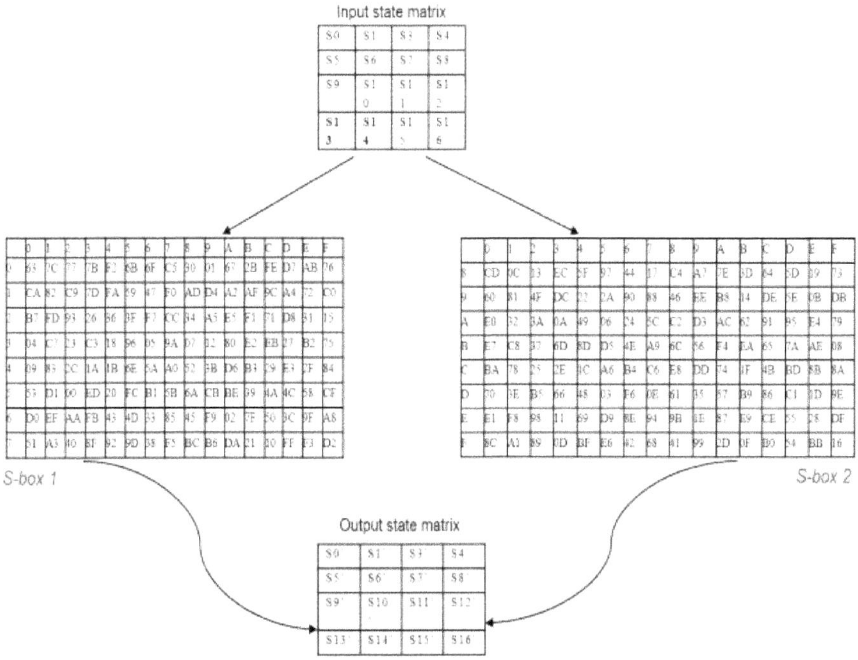

Figure 6.5: The proposed architecture for E-AES

6.3 EXPERIMENTATION AND RESULTS ANALYSIS

For the suggested EAES algorithm's implementation, the notion of multithreading was applied to provide parallel programming support. The experimental analysis is performed on the Linux platform, which provides C model-building capabilities. Two performance measures will be used to evaluate the proposed Enhanced-AES (EAES) algorithm: energy usage and execution time. In terms of running time and energy consumption, the suggested EAES algorithm will be compared to the standard AES version, which uses two threads for parallelism but does not partition the S-box. The proposed work will also be tested on a variety of multicore CPUs, including Intel core 2 duo, Intel i5, Intel i3, and Intel i7, with the results compared. Other symmetric encryption methods will be compared against our Enhanced-AES, including skipjack, RC5, and Blowfish.

6.3.1 Proposed E-AES Outcomes and comparative analysis

On a Linux platform, the execution time of the suggested E-AES algorithm is compared to that of the standard AES method. Figure 6.6 shows a running time comparison between the standard AES algorithm's multithreading concept without S-box dividing and the E-AES algorithm's multithreading concept with S-box splitting into two sections. The graph illustrates that the suggested E-AES requires less time to operate and that the running time lowers as we progress from low-end processor to high-end processors such as Intel core 2 duo, to Intel Core i3, to Intel core i5 to core i7 CPUs.

As the size of the input plaintext block rises, Figure 6.7 displays the execution time of the standard AES method and the suggested E-AES algorithm. The graph illustrates that the suggested E-AES technique works better as the number of input blocks increases from one to 50, with one block equaling 128 bits. It is also clearly understood form the figure that when more and more data is encrypted continuously the speed difference between the E-AES and standard AES algorithm also increases in the same proportion. Since sensor networks generate huge amount of data, which needs to be encrypted very frequently, so in the long run the proposed E-AES encryption algorithm will perform better and give results very fast as compared to standard AES algrothm.

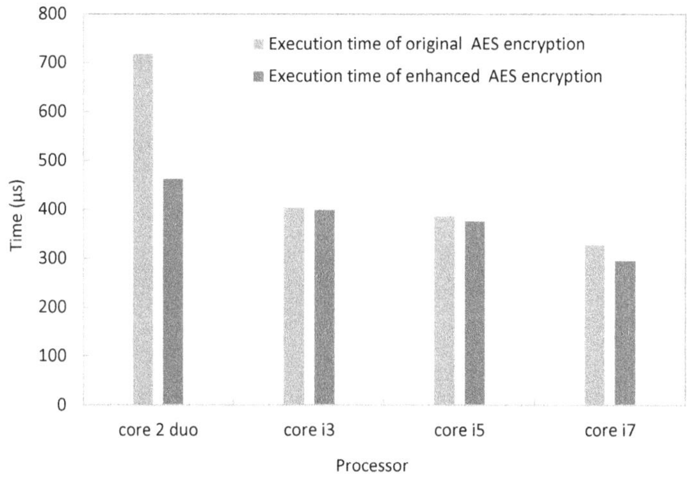

Figure 6.6: Execution time on different processors.

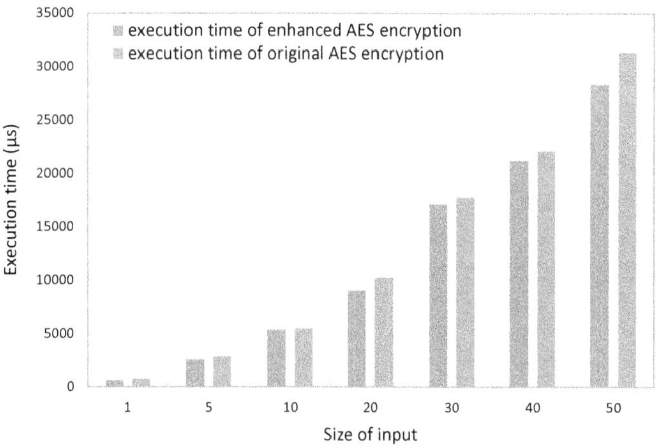

Figure 6.7: Time to execute vs. block size of input data (1 block = 128 bits)

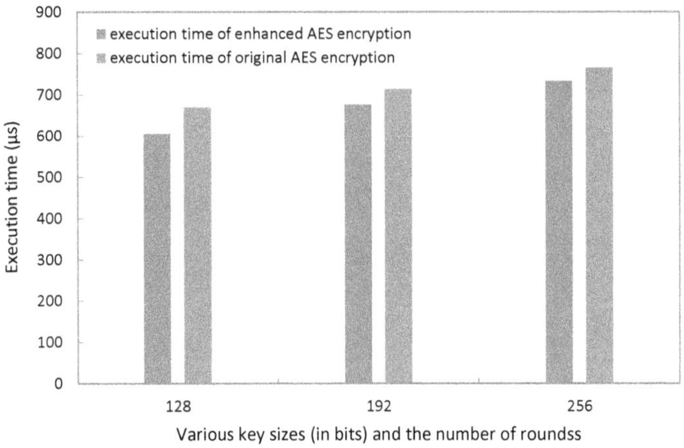

Figure 6.8: Time to execute versus number of rounds and key size

Figure 6.8 shows how conventional AES and EAES compare in terms of execution time for three different key sizes (128-bit key, 192-bit key, and 256-bit key) and the varied number of rounds. It takes ten rounds to encrypt the data with a 128-bit key, twelve rounds to encrypt the data with a 192-bit key, and fourteen rounds to encrypt the data with a 256-bit key. The graph clearly illustrates that the execution time of EAES improves over that of the original AES as the size of the key and the number of rounds rise. For 128-bit input block size, Figure 6.9 compares the suggested EAES encryption method to three other prominent symmetric encryption algorithms used in WSN: Skipjack, RC5, and Blowfish. Although the original AES method is slower than these three, it is more secure against assaults. Blowfish uses more memory and has weak keys than AES. RC5 uses less memory, but it is more prone to attacks. Skipjack is a rapid block encryption technique that is inefficient in WSNs. Using EAES, the time disparity between AES and the other three examined algorithms is decreased. The results confirmed the enhanced EAES' superior performance, demonstrating that it is a good alternative for encryption in WSN and security enhancement.

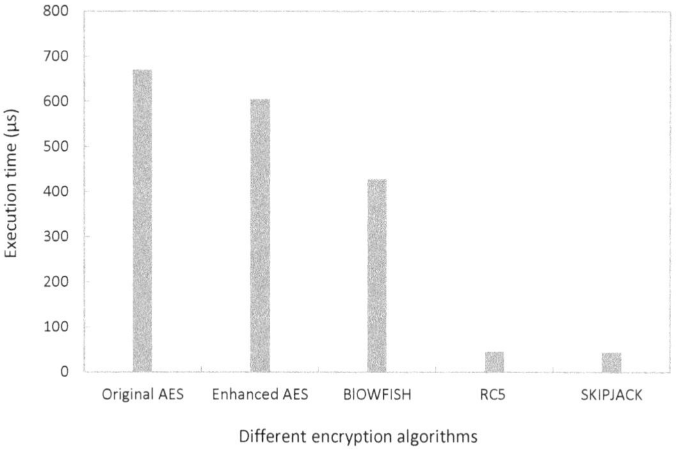

Figure 6.9: The execution times of the standard AES, E- AES, RC5, Skipjack and Blowfish

The suggested EAES and standard AES algorithms used the multithreading concept with two threads, however, if implemented on a machine with at least the same number of CPU cores as threads, increasing the number of threads and partitioning the S-box proportionally enhances performance. Performance degrades and execution time increases when multithreading is performed on a single CPU computer with no multiple cores or a machine with fewer CPU cores than threads. The experiment was carried out on an Intel Core2 Duo CPU, and when the number of threads rises from two to four, the execution time increases, this is depicted in Figure 6.10. It emphasizes how Enhanced-AES outperforms original AES for 2, 4, and 8 threads.

6.3.2 Analysis of power consumption

The suggested EAES algorithm energy utilization was calculated using a first-order radio model [83,84,85]. The following are the characteristics of the EAES algorithm that has been proposed: Table 6.1 shows the symbols and values used in the preceding equations.

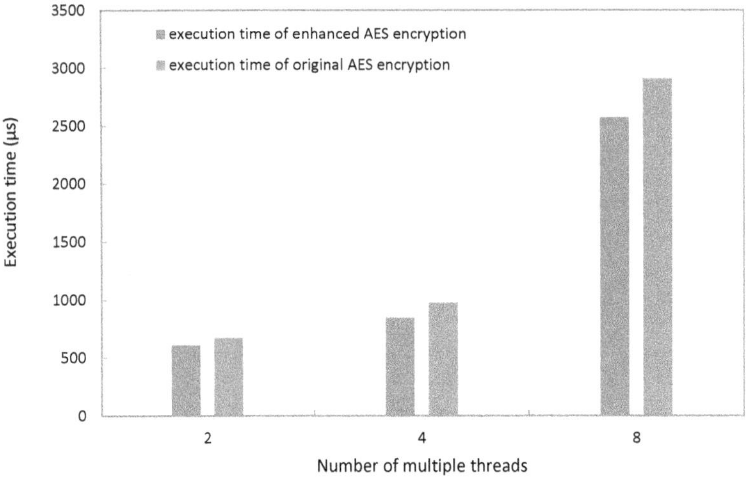

Figure 6.10: Time to execute vs. the number of threads

Table 6.1: Energy model symbols and default values

S.No.	Notations	Name of Symbol	Default Value
1.	E_{elec}	Electronics energy	50 nJ/bit
2.	ϵ_{amp}	Amplifier energy	0.1 nJ/bit/m^2
3.	E_p	Energy for processing	5 nJ/bit/cycle
4.	k	Message size	input data (in bits)
5.	d	Transfer distance	default 1-meter distance
6.	n	CPU cycles used	dependent on input data

The following equations

$$E_{Tx}(k,d) = E_{elec} \times k + \epsilon_{amp} * k * d^2 \qquad (6.1)$$

The amount of energy used by a sensor to receive a message:

$$E_{Rx}(k) = E_{elec} \times k \qquad (6.2)$$

The sensor's total energy consumption during processing:

$$E_{TP} = E_p \times n \times k \qquad (6.3)$$

Finally, the sensor node's total energy consumption:

$$E_{Total} = E_{Tx} + E_{Rx} + E_{TP} \qquad (6.4)$$

For various sizes of input data, Table 6.2 displays the value of CPU cycles,n, which is determined from the execution time for both the original AES and the proposed EAES.

Table 6.2: CPU cycles for EAES and original AES

S.No.	Size of input data in blocks (1 block = 128 bits)	CPU cycles (n) for proposed Enhanced-AES	CPU cycles (n) for Original Version of AES
1.	1	1.27E+06	1.41E+06
2.	5	5.41E+06	6.08E+06
3.	10	1.13E+07	1.15E+07
4.	20	1.90E+07	2.15E+07
5.	30	3.60E+07	3.73E+07
6.	40	4.45E+07	4.65E+07
7.	50	5.94E+07	6.58E+07

Figure 6.11 depicts the energy consumption with varied input block sizes, in the standard AES and the Enhanced-AES (EAES). It has been observed that EAES consumes less power than the original AES. The original AES's rate of energy consumption growth is faster than that of Enhanced AES. In a nutshell, the suggested EAES lowers sensor node power consumption by 11% while enhancing the sensor network's total lifespan.

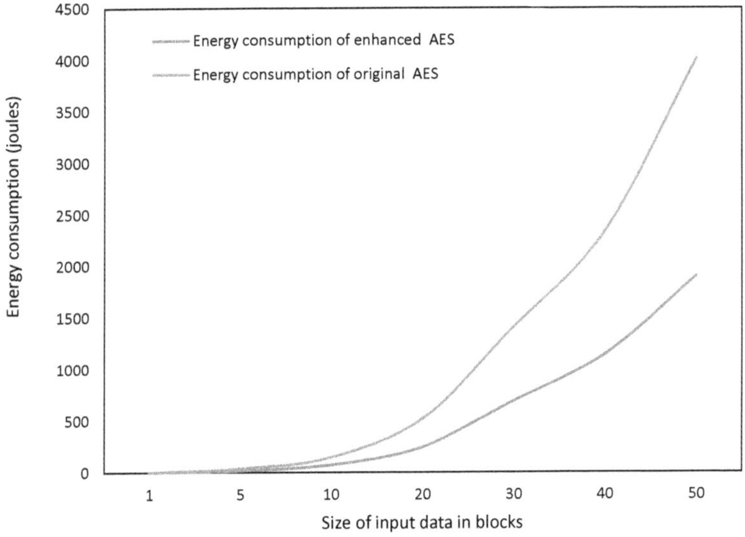

Figure 6.11: The Enhanced-AES algorithm's energy consumption as the input data size is increased.

6.4 SUMMARY

Our study focus is to reduce the execution time of the AES encryption algorithm by using the concept of a few strands running in line with the S-box separation. The AES S-box is divided into two parts so that two threads can access it simultaneously. This strategy improves the algorithm's execution time when compared to a multithreaded solution that does not use the concept of splitting. Other encryption methods utilized in sensor networks, such as RC5, Blowfish, and Skipjack, were also tested against our suggested Enhanced-AES (EAES) algorithm. The EAES method outperforms the traditional AES algorithm across a wide range of input key sizes, block sizes, and rounds. Because the EAES method requires fewer CPU cycles than the traditional AES, the power consumption is lowered by about 11%. In addition, if the size of the input data is large, the growth rate of EAES power consumption is lower than that of the original AES. As a result, the proposed EAES algorithm enhances the network length and performance of wireless sensor networks.

www.ingramcontent.com/pod-product-compliance
Lightning Source LLC
LaVergne TN
LVHW050822061126
851857LV00012B/924